A Stone's Throw

The Story of Steve Stone's Most Improbable Cy Young Season and the 1980 Baltimore Orioles

Bill Pemstein

Published by Bill Pemstein, Lake Zurich, Ill. First printing June 2011.

ISBN: 978-0-615-49320-6

Cover photo: Steve Stone pitches in Game 4 of the 1979 World Series in Pittsburgh. (Photo by Focus on Sport/Getty Images. Reprinted with permission.)

Table of Contents

Foreword

Flashback to 1980, three years before I became a very underpaid employee of my favorite sports team in the world. I was always madly in love with the Baltimore Orioles baseball team. The Birds did almost everything right in those days.

As in win, win, win and win some more. The Orioles had one losing season (1967) from when I was still playing Little League through my third season as an Orioles employee (1985).

From 1966 through 1983, no franchise saw more success than the Orioles. Only Oakland won as many World Series (three) during that time. The Orioles appeared in three more World Series and won two additional American League East titles. They also finished second seven times. Just once in that 18-year span did the Orioles finish below .500, 1967.

The Orioles were baseball's gold standard.

One thing the Orioles always had was pitching and defense. So why did they invest bucks on a very average pitcher named Steve Stone in 1979?

Steve Stone had just finished a 12-12 season with the White Sox in 1978. A year earlier, he won a career-high 15 games for the Chisox, no doubt aided by the offensive firepower the "South Side Hitmen" provided. Prior to that, Stone had a couple undistinguished years with the Cubs. His claim to fame was that he was one of the players included in the deal that sent Ron Santo from the Cubs to the South Side.

Then in 1980, Stone evidently sold his soul to the devil. There was really no other way to explain it. How else do you explain a pitcher winning 25 games one season after an undistinguished career in which, up to that point, he was one game under .500?

And one year after Stone reached the pinnacle, his career was over, a victim of arm injuries.

Orioles fans like me had their hearts broken in the 1979 World Series. I can still recall the *Washington Star* talking with the Pittsburgh players after the Pirates fell down three games to one in the Series. They said the Orioles were the best team they had ever seen.

Damn right, they were. And then the O's stopped hitting.

Steve Stone? A nobody in my book. We had Cy Young Award winners (Jim Palmer and Mike Flanagan). We had sure 20-game winners in Scott McGregor and Dennis Martinez. There was no room in this dazzling rotation for a lifetime losing pitcher like Stone.

In August 1980, I worked for the Voice of America in D.C. My life wasn't anything to write home about, but the Orioles were hot. I asked my friends to turn on the radio in the car. I said that Stone was pitching on the coast. It was the seventh inning, and he had a no-hitter going.

What the heck is going on?

Stone was also going for win No. 20. He had never won more than 15 games in any one season.

What the heck is going on?

It's an amazing story of how an average pitcher had the best single season in Orioles' history.

All this good news from the club from Baltimore inspired me to try to gain employment from them. I was hired in the winter of 1983 for $4.00 an hour.

After the 1983 World Series Championship, I began to sell group and season tickets to clients in the D.C. area. I met plenty of great folks as the Orioles began to fall back to Earth. The greatest team ever was suddenly a bad team.

So, after nearly five years working for the Orioles, I gave up a life in baseball and moved to the Chicago area. That's where I saw this Stone fellow again chatting about Cubs baseball on WGN. That's it, I thought, I will write a book about his magical year in Baltimore.

It's been a struggle. How do you write a book? Where was I going to find information for this project? The local library in Lake Zurich, Ill. was helpful. Matt Wagner helped me get articles from all the out-of-town newspapers when Stone pitched in 1980. I also scoured two of the best baseball websites, Retrosheet and Baseball Reference, to fact-check and find statistical trends. Those two sites are invaluable.

And then I made the trip back to Baltimore. In addition to seeing my great friends, I spent hours in the Enoch Pratt Library, photo-copying every stinking article from the *Baltimore Sun*. There was plenty of information to be had. I also got a hold of the old *Washington Posts*.

And then on the Sunday of that trip, I was the lone reporter in the auxiliary dugout of Camden Yards in Baltimore. There, I took my wife Eileen's tape recorder and asked as many members of the 1983 Orioles World Champion team as I could simply one question: How do you explain how Steve Stone won 25 games in one season? I got some great responses.

But I still had no answer from the hero of my book. Stone was nice enough to call me back but decided he didn't want to talk about it. But I set out to write it anyway. I wrote and e-mailed a query letter to everyone. I had some nice responses. A few folks asked to see some chapters. I was rejected plenty of places. I went a few rounds with publishers.

And then a fax came to my office at Pioneer Press a few years later. Former Cy Young Award winner Steve Stone would be signing autographs for $25 a piece in nearby Highland Park.

I was going for sure. Arriving with a few chapters from my book, I showed Stone what I had worked on. His agent asked for my card but Stone gave me a number to call him the next day. My interview wasn't great but I did get some good stuff from him.

A literary agent joined up with me and proceeded to try and sell it. Still, more dead ends. More than seven years have passed. It was time to publish this book.

Thanks to T.J. Brown of Northbrook, Ill., a former co-worker at Pioneer Press. A wordsmith at the top of his game, he helped prepare this book for baseball fans everywhere.

Bill Pemstein
May 2011
Lake Zurich, Ill.

Aug. 19, 1980

American League East	W	L	Pct.	GB
New York	71	46	.607	—
Baltimore	68	48	.586	2½
Milwaukee	66	54	.550	6½
Boston	60	54	.526	9½
Detroit	59	56	.513	11
Cleveland	59	57	.509	11½
Toronto	48	68	.414	22½

Pitching Matchup

Baltimore (Steve Stone 19-4, 3.01) at California (Alfredo Martinez 3-4, 5.05)

1

A 20-game winner

When the Orioles' bus pulled into Anaheim in the late afternoon on Aug. 19, not all of the players were aboard. For one, pitcher Steve Stone had taken an earlier charter plane following the exhausting Yankees series. The 33-year-old right-hander brought some company. He had purchased and planned to distribute three cases of bubbly for himself and his teammates.

The veteran of 10 Major League seasons was attempting to reach the 20-win plateau for the first time in his career that night against the struggling Angels. The last person to win 20 this early in the season was the Chicago White Sox's baffling Wilbur Wood in 1973. Wood, a rubber-armed knuckleballer, started 48 games that year, winning 24. In Orioles lore, the late Dave McNally also reached the 20-win mark in August 1970, but it was 11 days later than the day Stone would go for No. 20.

Stone, who had never won more than 15 games in any one season, took no chances. He brought out his A game to the Big A and proceeded to run through the Angels' batting attack. Early in this contest, the right-hander felt he had the stuff not only to win but throw a no-hitter as well.

"I was aware of the no-hitter right from the start," Stone told the *Baltimore Evening Sun.* "When I saw that big zero under the hit column on the scoreboard. And I was going for it from the second inning on. I felt I had the kind of stuff to pitch a no-hitter."

Baltimore catcher Dan Graham was thinking the same thing. That's why he scrapped Stone's fastball that night and concentrated on his pitcher's best offering — the curveball.

"Basically, I stayed away from the fastball," Graham said. "There was no way they could hit the curveball. He was throwing it at different speeds. He was throwing a wide one and one on the inside."

Stone retired the first 10 Halos before taking a second look at seven-time American League batting champion Rod Carew. He issued a free pass ending any dreams of a perfect game. Carew wasn't on base very long. Carney Lansford, who would win a batting title the next year, bounced one in the direction of Orioles' shortstop Mark Belanger. It was a quick 6-4-3 double play. Bobby Grich, a former Oriole who became one of Gene Autry's first big free agent signings in 1976, would earn a base on balls in the fifth inning, but the next batter, Larry Harlow, another ex-Oriole, took a called third strike. The no-hitter was alive in the sixth even when Stone reached for a Bert Campaneris dribbler, managing to deflect it. The ball had eyes, dancing to Belanger for a quick 1-6-3 out. Next, Rick Miller lined hard to Gary Roenicke in left to close the book on this frame.

The seventh was even easier. Carew flew out to Al Bumbry. Stone's fifth strikeout victim was Carney Lansford. Don Baylor punched a ball towards Belanger and took a seat after the sure-handed shortstop tossed him out. Stone was six outs away from immortality.

By the late innings this game was not in doubt. O's budding superstar Eddie Murray had rung up a 400-foot plus homer in the second inning, and in the seventh, Doug DeCinces reached Andy Hassler for a long ball. One inning later, catcher Graham found a Hassler pitch to his liking and also left the yard. In 83 innings in an Angels uniform, the southpaw Hassler surrendered just eight homers. However, 25 percent of his season total came in those two innings. With a five-run cushion, Stone could concentrate on his no-hit bid.

And then came the eighth inning. Stone's control deserted him. He issued consecutive one-out walks to Grich and Larry Harlow. Veteran Campaneris, in his 17th season in a Major League uniform, stepped up and lined a clean one-out single to center.

More than 25 years later, Stone knew exactly what happened to his no-hit bid.

"It was a 2-0 fastball to Bert Campaneris and he hit it up the middle," Stone told this writer.

The no-hitter was no more.

"I'm not a shutout pitcher," Stone told the *Los Angeles Times*. "The secret to my success has beengreat defense and our ability to score runs. I was thinking about the no-hitter from the second inning on, but I'm not disappointed that I didn't get it."

Pinch-hitter Dan Ford followed with a bloop single to center, knocking in a run, and chasing Stone out of the game as well.

"At that time when you face a pitcher coming in who's been pretty hot, you try to be more of a disciplined hitter," Ford, a former Orioles outfielder said. "There aren't that many chances you are going to get. His pitches were on. He didn't give you anything good to hit."

Manager Earl Weaver had seen enough of his latest star. He waved to the bullpen for the southpaw Tippy Martinez. Stone departed to the warm applause of the Angels fans.

Five outs later (two on strikeouts), Martinez had his ninth save, and Stone was in the Orioles record book. He had won his 20th game.

"When he finally figured he had a chance at the Cy Young Award, he was always around the relievers because we saved his games," Martinez said.

It was party time in the Orioles clubhouse. The Birds had flown to 21 games over the ..500 mark and stood just two games back in the loss column behind the Yankees in the pennant race of 1980. And Stone was sitting on 20 wins with more than a month to play. His only concern that night in Anaheim was the health of his champagne.

"The only thing I was worried about is that champagne doesn't travel well," Stone told the *Washington Post*. "I carted it all the way to Anaheim and I didn't want to take it to Oakland, too."

Stone was soon wearing his vintage grapes. Truthfully, he was more content to wear it than slurping the liquid.

"I hope the guys don't mind," Stone told *Newsweek*. "But I don't like champagne."

Hard feelings aside, third baseman Doug DeCinces turned over a bottle and deposited on Stone's head.

"How long have you been waiting for this," DeCinces inquired with a *Sun* reporter watching .

"Ten years," Stone replied. "And it sure feels good."

"And how many starts have you got?" asked right fielder Ken Singleton.

Simple mathematics told the tale. Stone had 11 more possible starts.

"Steve looks like he doesn't think he's ever going to lose another game," added shortstop Mark Belanger.

Pitching coach Ray Miller brought up the confidence factor.

"It's uncanny the confidence he has," Miller said. "He came in here today with 36bottles of champagne. He hands them to the clubhouse boy and says, 'Ice them up, kid.'

"Now, that's a guy who doesn't expect to lose. I've seen pitchers who got stuck on 19 and winning the 20th really became a phobia. Steve just buzzed through it."

Spring training of 1980 was cruel to Weaver and the defending American League champs from Baltimore. On March 25, starter Dennis Martinez tore a deltoid muscle in his right shoulder sending him to the disabled list. The 25-year-old right-hander would miss the first 10 days of the regular season. He would win only six of his 245 career victories in this campaign.

Scott McGregor would also be sidelined by opening day. Tendonitis put the lefty on the shelf for the first two weeks of the regular season. In this case, it only made the ex-Yankee farmhand work harder. In 1980, McGregor would register his lone 20-win campaign during his 13 seasons in orange and black.

No one could have expected that Stone's 1980 season would stun the baseball world. The Euclid, Ohio native would win 25 games, making him the lone 25-game winner of the entire 1980s in the Majors.

He led the American League in winning percentage (.781) with his 25-7 mark.

After a slow start, Stone won 23 of his last 27 decisions.

He won 14 straight decisions from May 9 to July 26. He was the 12th pitcher in American League history to win 14 straight games.

Stone defeated every AL club at least once. And he retired all nine National League starters in the All-Star Game. He won more games in a single season than any other Orioles pitcher in club history. He was selected the AL Cy Young Award winner.

And 12 starts later in 1981 his season and career were over.

"For the first time, it all came clear," Stone told *Newsweek*. "It was as if a TV picture had been jumping around and I finally figured out how to adjust the horizontal."

His teammates went along for this joyous ride.

"It was amazing," said Orioles outfielder Ken Singleton. "We thought he had sold his soul to the devil. If you put money on him winning 25 games you would have been retired and living in a penthouse. You can ask most Orioles fan who is the biggest single-season winner in club history and most will say Jim Palmer."

O's outfielder Gary Roenicke also recalled Stone's stunning romp.

"That particular year for Steve, he put everything together." Roenicke said. "He had a great, great curveball. He was healthy. We played good defense behind him. We gave him some runs. He had confidence in us and vice verse. Every time he went out we knew he would pitch a good game."

Six-foot-7 reliever Tim Stoddard saved 9 of those wins for Stone in 1980.

"He had the year of his life and helped us achieve our goals," Stoddard said.

"To see a guy have that type of year is pretty impressive. This is what makes the game great. If it was predictable it wouldn't be much fun."

Tippy Martinez had a pair of saves during Stone's improbable run.

"You couldn't get a better year than that," Martinez said. "I was fortunate enough to see something like that in my lifetime. Steve was good but with the combination of defense and he doing the things he was capable of doing. Things kind of came into place for Steve. Everything went right."

Orioles infielder Lenn Sakata remembers seeing plenty of curveballs that season.

"It was just a phenomenal season," Sakata said. "A no-brainer season. I think it happens if you have the opportunity to play long enough. Everyone has it in them at the Major League level. It was a career year. The next year, he blows out and that's it."

To this day, former general manager Hank Peters remains incredulous when recalling this incredible campaign of the 32-year-old right-hander.

"We knew he would be a good pitcher," Peters said. "But win 25 games? There aren't that many people who do that. I don't care how good they are. A lot of good pitchers haven't won 20 games. For him to win 25, he had one of those seasons where he was un-hittable. We signed him because we thought he would be a good pitcher. Did we think he would win 25 games? No. The fact that he did it makes all of us look good.

"It was one of those things where you can't really explain it. I don't know that he can. He had a great curveball. Even though the hitters in certain situations felt they could hit it, they still couldn't hit it."

Twenty-three years later, Stone fully admitted he was not the most likely of candidates to win 25 games in a single season.

"I can name 50 Orioles pitchers better than me," Stone said. "Even 100. I might be the least likely to do it. I was really 5-foot-9 1/4. So, I was a sub 6-foot starter. That was one hurdle. The odds today of making it in a rotation are slim and none. Everything had to line up perfectly. It probably couldn't happen today."

When the White Sox right-hander signed with the Orioles after the 1978 season, his agent added a clause to his contract that his client would receive a $10,000 bonus (that was a considerable addition to his salary in those days), in any year he won the Cy Young Award. But as everyone in the baseball world fully knew, Steve Stone was never going to win a Cy Young Award in any year.

"I think it was something my agent just threw in there," Stone told *The New York Times*. "I don't think he thought it was a serious proposal. I didn't. A bonus for a winning season would have made more sense. It was like an insurance salesman telling you, 'We'll give you $50,000 if an elephant falls on you,' because he knows darn well an elephant isn't going to fall on you."

Stone credits his special campaign in Baltimore for paving the way to his second career as a baseball broadcaster in the Midwest.

"I'm forever the 1980 Cy Young Award winner," Stone said. "And all these years later, I'm still on TV. That's still a nice perk. That's ABC, *Monday Night Baseball* and Harry Caray's partner. I needed that first step, that opportunity. It was a vindication of sorts."

This wasn't Chicago. This wasn't some run of the mill team. The Orioles of the late 1970s and early 1980s were contenders every year.

"I can't deny that wearing a Baltimore uniform has made a big difference," Stone said. "I would have liked to play my whole career in Baltimore but you can't look back.

"For one reason or another, nobody ever wanted to give me the ball without having a string attached to it. If I pitched well for three starts, then had the fourth, I wouldn't get the fifth start because I didn't have the stamina. I wasn't big enough, they said, I was getting tired."

Orioles fans of today may not believe it, but at this time, the Orioles organization was the envy of baseball. From 1964 to 1983, the Orioles finished lower than third just twice. Once was a sub-.500 season as defending World Champions in 1967. The other was a 90-win effort in 1978 that was nine games worse than Boston and New York.

"That is the glaring difference in a winning organization like Baltimore and the ones that don't win. Before they get a ballplayer, they study him thoroughly. They didn't know whether I'd win any games for them but they knew I wouldn't be trouble. If you aren't a plus, at least you aren't a minus."

It was clearly a dream season for the right-hander. If only his team had won a few more games.

"I've always looked at this award as something that someone was supposed to win. A great season has always eluded Steve Stone in the past. I could never put six good months together in one season before 1980. But I feel good about this. If you were to write down a script for this year and put down everything you could possibly want to happen, it would unfold just like this."

Baltimore Orioles 1980 Rotation

1979 Statistics

Player	W	L	ERA	G	IP	H	BB	SO
Mike Flanagan	23	9	3.08	39	265⅔	245	70	190
Jim Palmer	10	6	3.30	23	155⅔	144	43	67
Dennis Martinez	15	16	3.66	40	292⅓	279	78	132
Scott McGregor	13	6	3.35	27	174⅔	165	23	81
Steve Stone	11	7	3.77	32	186	173	73	96

Career Statistics (through 1979)

Player	W	L	ERA	G	IP	H	BB	SO
Mike Flanagan*	60	40	3.63	137	876⅔	843	266	569
Jim Palmer***	225	122	2.66	447	3275⅓	2691	1092	1927
Dennis Martinez	46	36	3.67	126	763	716	243	399
Scott McGregor	31	25	3.57	94	536⅓	518	105	236
Steve Stone	78	79	4.06	268	1475	1420	588	886

*Denotes number of Cy Young Awards won through 1979 season.

2

Long odds

It wasn't a great night for sleeping anyway. It had been a rocky Sunday. Early that crisp morning, Stone had been tipped off that a 5.1 earthquake in Washington state had had ignited Mount St. Helens. He tried to comprehend how nearly 230 square miles of forest below the volcano had been destroyed. It wasn't a good day for his team, either.

When teammate Al Bumbry doubled in a pair of runs in the eighth inning in Detroit, the Orioles had overtaken the Tigers and taken a 4-3 lead. And McGregor was pitching well, so six more outs and an Orioles win were good bets before the road trip continued to Cleveland. Both Tim Stoddard and Tippy Martinez pitched in the bottom of the eighth frame as Detroit scored three times to overtake Baltimore 6-4. It was the Orioles 19th loss of the campaign, and now the defending American League champs were five games under the .500 mark on May 18.

At the Bond Hotel in Cleveland that night, Stone settled in late that night to engage that Indians lineup in his mind. He felt sure he would face leadoff hitter Miguel Dilone. In many ways, these two players from different worlds were going through a similar renaissance of their baseball careers. Dilone would have the best season of his 12-year career, hitting .340. But of course, in his mind, Stone would throw that slow breaking ball and get this speedster to tap out to Murray at first.

And so it went. Duane Kuiper was next. And yes, Stone had heard all the jokes before. He knew he was the punch line rather the answer to this trivia question. Name the only pitcher in baseball history to allow a home run to Duane Kuiper?. That answer is simply Steve Stone. In this pitcher-perfect dream, Stone kept his fastball away and made Kuiper bounce out to Garcia who made a decent play.

Mike Hargrove was next and Stone did not allow the "Human Rain Delay" to annoy him. He waited patiently for Hargrove to step in the box and then would tease him with curves away and fastballs in tight. Stone could visualize the big pop-up settling safely in Murray's glove ending the first inning.

Big Cliff Johnson would be next. Slow, slower and slowest to this giant. Stone visualized this 33-year-old slugger fanning at most every pitch he threw. The Indians would send up another left-handed bat at Stone in catcher Ron Hassey.

This was an easy mental exercise. Stone never had any trouble from Hassey in the first place. He would change speeds and move it inside and outside and dispense of this lefty hitter.

Toby Harrah would score 100 runs for the 1980 Indians. But lifetime, in more than 30 at-bats, this one-time All-Star hit less than .200 off of Stone. He dispensed this third baseman easily during this mind session.

Stone had seen enough of part-time outfielder Ron Pruitt. In this sequence, he fooled Pruitt with a steady diet of breaking balls. Stone's book on lefty batter Del Alston was similar. He doubted

Alston could adjust to the slowest of his benders. Shortstop Tom Veryzer could simply be overpowered. He was not a threat to hurt Stone in any way.

And so it went through the morning hours of May 19. Stone would retire all of these hitters in order and make national news with yet another perfect game.

It was just a dream but this kind of mental preparation paved the way for his enormous success in 1980.

"I used to try not to lose before," he told Henry Hecht of the *New York Post* before taking the mound and starring in the 1980 All-Star Game in Los Angeles. "Now, when I go out, I go out to win every time, and I'm certain I am. I try to envision myself literally walking off the mound a winner. I allow no negatives in my thinking. When certain ones start creeping in, I erase them and make it like a blank blackboard waiting to be filled in with things like, 'The team is going to play well, is going to score some runs, I'm going to throw strikes, I'm going to win.' "

If his arm would hold out for a full season, Stone's ability to out-think his opponents might actually work.

"Concentration is the answer of course," Stone told *Sports Illustrated*. "In fact no one who has played this game has ever said it was anything less than 80 percent mental. Yet while every team has a trainer to care for the body, none has a specialist to administer to the mind. I try to reprogram my subconscious, sweep out all the negative feelings before every game. It's a self-psych that can come across as cocky but it works."

Stone seized an opportunity in spring training. His first spring outing vs. Texas on March 11 produced a four-hit three-inning performance. He allowed just two hits and struck out four in four innings of work against New York on March 15 at the Louisiana Superdome. A solo homer to Jim Spencer was the Yankees lone run off of Stone. This Yankees team had touched Hall-of-Famer Jim Palmer for eight runs over the first five innings.

"That's as good a velocity as I had all of last year," Stone told the *Baltimore Sun*. "Last year when I came here, I was trying to prove to everyone that I was worth what they paid me. And I tried to do it all in one month. The harder I threw, the worse I got. This year, I just feel very confident."

On March 20, Stone again took on the Texas Rangers and spell-bounded them for four innings. A six-run fifth inning drove him out. A two-run wind-blown homer from Bump Wills was the key blow.

"I just ran out of gas," Stone told the *Sun*. "I was still making good pitches in the fifth inning. I had hurt my back earlier in the spring and lost some time running. But I consider it a moral victory because I got John Grubb out for the first time in my life."

Stone wasn't exaggerating much. If every pitcher was Steve Stone, Grubb could well visit his plaque in baseball's Hall of Fame. Five times in his 16-year career, Grubb had three or more hits off of Stone in a game. He finished with a shiny .409 mark in 44 trips to the plate against Stone.

Stone's line for this exhibition game wasn't pretty:

IP	H	R	ER	BB	K
5	10	8	8	3	3

Despite the ugly numbers, Manager Weaver had seen enough positives from the 32-year-old to comment.

"It's the survival of the fittest," Weaver told the *Sun*. "I hate to sound callous but I have to put the healthiest arms in the rotation. Dennis (Martinez) has pitched well but if he's sore, I'll put Stone in there."

Weaver never seemed to worry about spring training records, but the 1980 Grapefruit League season produced an unsightly 7-14 re-cord after an eight-game losing streak. Stone took the loss in an 8-2 loss to the Reds on March 29. He allowed three earned runs in five innings of work.

The 1979 Orioles fell one game short of a dream season. Come-from-behind victories were commonplace as the Birds won 12 more games than the year before and posted the Majors' best record (102-57). Like most winning Orioles clubs, it was built on pitching and defense. The veteran staff had the reigning Cy Young Award winner in lefty Mike Flanagan. If you count the 27-year-old's victory over the Angels in the 1979 playoffs and his win in Game One of the World Series vs. Pittsburgh he, too would have been a 25-game winner. But Flanagan was coming off a 19-win campaign the year before. He didn't take anyone by surprise when he landed his Cy Young Award. In July of 1979, Flanagan stood at 10-6 with an ERA of more than four runs per game. With his overhand curve and rising fastball, the southpaw won 13 of his next 16 decisions with a 2.22 ERA and 10 complete games.

He won the Cy Young Award easily. Flanagan racked up 26 first-place votes. Out of the running with one vote each came New York Yankees teammates Tommy John and Ron Guidry. Guidry, "Louisiana Lightning," was one year removed from his 25-win campaign in 1978.

In James Alvin Palmer, the Orioles had a three-time Cy Young Award winner and a future Hall-of-Famer.

While Stone was contemplating his baseball plans at Kent State University, Palmer was outdueling Sandy Koufax in Game Two of the 1966 World Series.

It's a little known fact that any club could have snatched Palmer from the Birds in 1967.

His right wing wasn't well, and he spent much of 1967 and 1968 in the minor leagues and on the disabled list. The organization might have been justified in giving up on him.

Instead, Palmer posted eight 20-win seasons in a Baltimore uniform. At nearly 6-foot-4, this handsome performer simply had more natural skill than his latest teammate, Stone. The big leg kick and the overhand fastball to go with it, Palmer collected his first Cy Young in

1973 in a tight election over the California Angels' Nolan Ryan. Two years later, he again piled up more votes than runner-up Catfish Hunter. His final Cy Young came in 1976. It also marked his easiest margin of victory over the Tigers' wunderkind Mark Fidrych.

Palmer also notched an 8-4 record while pitching in the postseason, his last win coming in relief in the pivotal Game Three of the 1983 World Series. Palmer would never win another game in the Major Leagues after that win at Veterans Stadium. He would go 0-3 before being released in 1984. In 1991, he attempted a comeback a year after being inducted in the Hall of Fame. A hamstring injury forced Palmer to call it off before the Orioles left Fort Lauderdale.

Just prior to the 1991 comeback, Palmer was loosening up at the University of Miami, where he caught the attention of Miami assistant coach Lazaro Callazo, according to *Sports Illustrated*. Callazo went over to offer some advice.

"You'll never make the Hall of Fame with those mechanics," Callazo said.

Palmer didn't have to worry. His comeback didn't pan out, but he was already enshrined in Cooperstown two years earlier.

Lefty Scott McGregor was selected in the first round of the 1972 amateur baseball draft by the Yankees. Four years later, he was thrown in that memorable deal that sent catcher Rick Dempsey, reliever Tippy Martinez and starter Rudy May from the Yanks to Baltimore for Ken Holtzman, Doyle Alexander, Grant Jackson, the beloved Ellie Hendricks and Jimmy Freeman.

New York was on the money for drafting McGregor first in the draft and completely wrong in sending him to the Orioles. He would win 138 games in an Orioles uniform and 28 in the two seasons combined prior to his best campaign, 1980.

McGregor didn't overpower American League hitters. Instead, the stylish southpaw would dazzle with a Stone-like curveball and a tricky motion.

Dennis Martinez would never win 20 games during his improbable 23-year career in the big leagues. But the first Nicaraguan in the Majors did put up 16-win and 15-win seasons prior to the 1980 campaign. Martinez's career could be told in three acts. Act I would be prior to the 1983 season, in which he was a young pitcher who consistently put up double-digit wins totals. Act II was the middle years of his career in which he lost his way, struggled to stay healthy and soon was dumped by Baltimore. Act III was Martinez's renaissance with Montreal, Cleveland and later Atlanta in which he became one of the game's best pitchers at that time. Martinez didn't retire until after the 1998 season after appearing in 53 games as a reliever and spot starter for Bobby Cox's Braves.

The Orioles were loaded with strong front-line pitching. And adding a homer-happy pitcher like Stone was a risky proposition. After all, Stone gave up 24 home runs with the Cubs in 1975, 25 with the White Sox in 1977, 19 with the White Sox in 1978 and 31 in 1979 with Baltimore.

Stone made his regular season pitching debut in Chicago on April 12. He matched young Richard Dotson with four scoreless innings. In chilly Chicago, Stone couldn't bring out his usual assortment of curveballs. Through five innings only an Alan Bannister run-producing bounce-out to Belanger kept him from a shutout. The sixth inning was a complete nightmare. Stone was only partially responsible. He hung a forkball to Orioles-killer Lamar Johnson and the Sox went up 2-0.

"I just made a bad pitch and he hit it," Stone said as reported by the *Baltimore Sun*. "It was too cold for any curveballs. The only success I had all day was with my fastball. I didn't have that real good sharp curve ball that I've had before."

Chet Lemon slapped a Stone pitch into center field and that ended Stone's outing. Before this sixth inning was closed, both Tippy Martinez and Joe Kerrigan made appearances. And both Johnson and Lemon batted again and laced run-scoring singles.

Seven runs and six hits would go up on the board and the Orioles were down 8-0. Only a two-run, ninth inning double by DeCinces would keep the O's from total embarrassment.

Stone's first outing of his magical 1980 season was an 8-2 loss.

On this night, the 21-year-old Dotson looked more like the Cy Young Award winner.

He even impressed the losing pitcher.

"He had a great straight change-up today," Stone told the *Chicago Tribune*. "And he wasn't afraid to throw it when he was behind the count. He had our hitters swinging from their front feet all day and that set up his fastball. If he can stay around the plate and can throw the change, he'll be awfully tough. He pitched like a 10-year veteran against us."

Stone's gaze at Dotson's crystal ball had some validity. The youngster would win 12 games in 1980 and 22 more in 1983, as a big part of the White Sox' 1983 American League West Championship. However, injuries stymied Dotson, and his 12-year-run closed in 1990, leaving him two games under .500.

Stone heard a discussion between his manager Earl Weaver and the local press after the loss to the White Sox. It may have sparked a change in his way of thinking.

"I never gave Earl any credit for understanding pitching," Stone told this writer. "After I had lost to the White Sox, he went to the press and said, 'Did you see that guys? That's 20-win stuff.'

"Nobody had ever said my stuff was 20-game stuff. I read that. The most I had ever won was 15. I wasn't about to dispute that fact. Did I know what was coming? Lord knows, no."

Stone took the mound at Memorial Stadium on April 17 versus Kansas City's hard-throwing Rich Gale. As Stone soon became used to during his improbable season, the Orioles offense awakened early for him. In the opening frame, shortstop Kiko Garcia stood on second base with two outs. He trotted home in front of Eddie Murray's two-run homer into the right-center field bleachers.

It was 2-0 because second-sacker Frank White was a tad greedy in the opening frame. He tried his luck running against Dempsey and soon found himself on the bench after being tossed out at second. What made matters worse for the visitors, George Brett followed with a booming opposite field two-bagger.

In the fourth, Pat Kelly's triple helped increase the margin to 3-0. Lowenstein followed with a hit to right field and Stone was up 4-0. Al Bumbry had a solo homer in the sixth and Stone kept on about his business.

"Pitching and homers," manager Weaver noted. "It's the old 1-2 punch. The best way to win."

In the home half of the sixth, he fanned Frank White and induced league MVP Brett to line out to Singleton in right. The inning concluded in timely fashion when Hal McRae grounded out to third baseman Floyd Rayford, who was making his Major League debut in this game. Rayford, a stocky infielder who would start and finish his playing days in an Orioles uniform, would peak with a 21-double, 18-homer and a .521 slugging percentage in 1985.

In 1980, Brett flirted most of the summer with the .400 mark. Stone had held the slugger to a double, walk and the aforementioned line drive to Singleton's glove, when Brett came up again with runners on the corners in the eighth. Stone elected to face Brett and paid for it as the future Hall-of-Famer bashed a ball past Singleton for a three-bagger. The hook came out and in came Stoddard. And other than a free pass issued to Willie Mays Aikens, the 6-foot-7 reliever was perfect.

Stone registered win No. 1, 5-2.

"Early last year, I had a natural adjustment period," Stone told the *Sun* that night. "I was kind of pitching to justify my contract every time I went out there. I had always been with a losing ballclub where all you have are your statistics. I had to learn in terms of 'we' instead of 'I'. I would feel upset when Earl pulled me early last year. But now, I'm more comfortable in my role, and I hope to get off to a little better start than 6-7."

Manager Weaver found little to complain about Stone's first two outings of the season.

"He pitched a fine game in Chicago," Weaver said. "This was the same kind of game actually. He had given up only 2 runs when his dummy manager went out and got him out of there. After he left, they (White Sox) broke it wide open."

Stone emerged the winner despite feeling the effects of a pulled hamstring. Manager Weaver noted the mild injury to Stone and scratched him from an upcoming start in New York.

"The leg is bothering him and he probably wouldn't have pitched in the Yankee series anyway," Weaver said. "So, a couple of days rest might do him some good."

Stone took the mound April 25 in Kansas City to try and stop the bleeding. The defending league champions had dropped the final two games of the White Sox series and then dropped three straight one-run games at Yankee Stadium. What made matters worse, two of those defeats came in New York's last at-bats. A trip to the Midwest was in order after this poor showing.

In KC, Stone was opposed by the crafty right-hander Larry Gura. It wasn't close. The Royals actually hit for a cycle in the first inning, andStone would face just 11 Royals hitters on this evening.

Willie Wilson doubled over Bumbry's head to open the home half of the first. Frank White dropped one in front of Roenicke in left and the fleet-footed Wilson (79 steals) breezed home for a lightning-quick 1-0 lead. George Brett smashed a ball to right that skidded on the artificial turf at Royals Stadium for a run-scoring triple. Stone recorded one out when Willie Aikens hit Murray in the glove at first base and the Hall-of-Famer trotted to the bag. Brett stood his ground on third base.

No matter, Hal McRae chased Brett home with run No. 3 with a clean double past Roenicke. Stone could have been spared further trouble with some help from his friends.

After striking out John Wathan, he had Pete LaCock hit the ball right at the sure-handed Dauer. The second-sacker would make only six errors all season in nearly 700 chances. His boot on this play would keep the inning going much to the delight of "can't-miss" prospect Clint Hurdle. Sure, he was supposed to be a true star but the records show Hurdle averaged 3.2 homers a season during his 10-year Big League career. And since he had no "power" on the base paths (one career steal), it wasn't a magical run through the Majors for Hurdle the player, 27 years before he skippered the Colorado Rockies to a World Series on the heels of a magical 20-1 run leading up to losing four straight to the Red Sox.

Hurdle decided this game with one swing. His three-run homer turned the game ugly early for the visitors from Baltimore. Manager Weaver didn't wait too long to see how this tale would end. He witnessed Stone surrendering a one-out single to White and issuing a free pass to Brett. And then Weaver reached for his hook.

In Stone's defense, this was his first outing in eight days.

"I was very strong," Stone said. "But I couldn't get the ball where I wanted it. I don't know what it was."

The 7-0 loss left Stone with a 1-2 mark. It seemed he never had a chance. The 1979 American League champions made four errors in this debacle. They managed just four singles off Gura.

Stone was nowhere to be seen. However, the Orioles hitters were just waiting around to be heard from. Stone's next start would come on the last day of April at home. The first-place Bronx Bombers were in town for a brief two-game set with the Birds.

The O's (6-11) had dropped 8 of its previous 9 contests and stood in fifth place. To make matters worse, it rained in Baltimore. New York's starter, Tom Underwood, would figure prominently in the Steve Stone success story of 1980. Exactly one-third of all of his losses (9) came at the hands of the O's right-hander.

Loss No. 1 for the southpaw was of the painless variety, ashe never got out of the second inning. After a 1-2-3 first inning, all was well for Underwood and the Yanks.

Then he walked Murray. One out later, DeCinces ripped his fourth homer of the young season to make it a 2-0 game. The Birds weren't through. Roenicke pulled one past Oscar Gamble in left for two bags. By the time Murray batted again in the same frame, the O's had scored six times, aided by two Yankees errors and a Bumbry run-scoring single.

Murray's second at-bat of the inning came against hard-throwing Ron Davis. Davis would later become the Minnesota relief ace in the mid-1980s, but Murray menaced him throughout his career, going 13 -for-28 (.464) with three homers and nine RBI. The first time the two faced each other, in August 1979, Billy Martin called in Davis to relieve Tommy John, face Murray and preserve a 6-4 lead. Murray promptly hit a two-run double, and then scored the go-ahead run on the next play.

This time, the Hall-of-Famer from the class of 2003, dropped a ball in front of Reggie Jackson in right scoring Dauer.

"We did score quite often with him (Stone)," noted former Orioles second baseman Rich Dauer. "We scored early in the game. He was the kind of pitcher who got the ball and knew what to do. We were very good behind pitchers like that."

Stone disputes the idea that the O's scored a dozen runs every time he took his turn in the rotation.

"I don't think that's accurate," Stone said. "They have said for a long time that they bombed away but there were plenty of 4-1, 4-2 games."

A closer examination supports Stone's claims. With its .273 team batting average, Baltimore placed fifth in the league in average trailing Texas, Boston, Cleveland and Milwaukee. In the 37 Stone starts, the O's inched that average to .277 (307 hits in 1,110 at bats).

Bumbry enjoyed his best overall season and sparked the team in hits, runs, singles, triples, and stolen bases saved his best for those 37 contests. He hit .318 for the season but a resounding .377 when Stone began the game on the mound. Murray hit 25 points higher but deposited just six of his 32 homers in Stone games.

That all said, Baltimore averaged 5.7 runs per Stone start, which was a full half-run per game better than what Stone got from the "South Side Hit Men" in 1977. The bullpen also did not lose any games for Stone in 1980, but managed to help him earn four wins. Stone would throw his last pitch with the Orioles tied or trailing, watch the Orioles get the lead in the next half of the inning, and see the bullpen close out the game.

The run support might not have mattered much. Stone had only two "cheap wins," which is any win in which a starter goes less than six innings or allows more than three earned runs. The league average of cheap wins is two.

Steve Stone Career Statistics

Through 1979

Yr	Club	W	L	ERA	G	IP	H	BB	SO
1971	San Francisco	5	9	4.15	24	110⅔	110	55	63
1972	San Francsisco	6	8	2.98	27	123⅔	97	49	85
1973	Chicago (AL)	6	11	4.24	36	176⅓	163	82	138
1974	Chicago (NL)	8	6	4.14	38	169⅔	185	64	90
1975	Chicago (NL)	12	8	3.95	33	214⅓	198	80	139
1976	Chicago (NL)	3	6	4.08	17	75	70	21	33
1977	Chicago (AL)	15	12	4.51	31	207⅓	228	80	124
1978	Chicago (AL)	12	12	4.37	30	212	196	84	118
1979	Baltimore	11	7	3.77	32	186	173	73	96
Totals		78	79	4.06	268	1475	1420	588	886

Postseason

Yr	Club	Series	W	L	ERA	G	IP	H	BB	SO
1979	Baltimore	WS	0	0	9.00	1	2	4	2	2

3

Nothing special

Brewers catcher Charlie Moore hit precisely five homers from 1977 though 1979. His one career tater off of Stone came on national television. With 30,000 fans viewing it in person at County Stadium, Stone dueled Jim Slaton before a Monday Night audience on July 30, 1979. Slaton retired the first nine Orioles he faced that night. Stone allowed no singles, doubles or triples. His one mistake popped up in the third when Moore wrapped one around the foul pole for a solo homer. That was the only hit the Brewers would manage against Stone. Don Money walked with two outs in the ninth breaking a string of 19 consecutive.

"I gave up that homer to Charlie Moore and took the one-hitter until there were two outs in the ninth," Stone told this writer. "I had Don Money down 0-2 and missed with a curve ball. I missed with four straight. Cecil Cooper was up and he (Weaver) had Tippy in the bullpen. Weaver asked me if I could get Cooper. I said, 'Of course not.' He brought in Tippy and Cooper flied out to left field and I just got a win."

Stone entered the 1980 season with a career mark of 78-79. He broke into the majors at age 23 and had the good fortune to play for the San Francisco Giants. That 1971 club won the Western Division of the National League with 90 victories before losing to the Pittsburgh Pirates in the 1971 National League Championship Series.

The Giants had made the Euclid, OH native their fourth pick of the 1969 Amateur Draft. As a rookie, Stone made 19 starts for the Giants. His first Major League decision stood out. It was a complete-game shutout over Roberto Clemente and the Pirates on April 23. The rematch between Stone and the Pirates was May 5. And in the third inning, Stone fanned Clemente, Willie Stargell and Richie Hebner. The bullpen failed him, however, and Stone sustained the first loss of his career. On May 19, he made his Wrigley Field debut. He would later appear in 88 games for the Cubs in the mid-1970s.His first outing in Chicago was not a happy one. Billy Williams and J.C. Martin went yard and Stone did not survive the second inning.

Stone's first season produced a 5-9 record with a disappointing 4.15 ERA. The losing trend continued into the 1972 campaign. Despite some strong outings, Stone opened the new campaign with four straight defeats. On May 24, Stone made one run stand up and scattered eight Dodgers hits in tossing a shutout. It ended a personal eight-game losing streak.

He promptly won his next two starts. On June 10, he would surrender ninth inning homers to Rick Monday and Ron Santo to fall to the Cubs. The winner of that one was Ferguson Jenkins, who would also be his mound opponent when the Rangers of 1980 broke Stone's personal 14-game winning streak. Stone was exiled to the bullpen in the latter part of the 1972 season,

Even with the ups and downs in 1972, Stone posted the best ERA of his career (2.98), even with a mediocre 6-8 record. On Nov. 29, 1972, Stone and teammate Ken Henderson (who scored 104 runs in 1970) were traded to the Chicago White Sox for right-handed pitcher Tom Bradley. On a Sox team that included future 1980 Yankees Bucky Dent and Goose Gossage, Stone didn't register his first American League victory until June 7. And it came in Memorial Stadium as he beat Jim Palmer and the Birds, 3-2.

Stone's best outing of the 1973 campaign may have been on the final day of the season. He struck out 12 Oakland hitters and fired a three-hitter in a 1-0 victory in 10 innings. His final record was 6-11 with an ERA of 4.24. Stone would finish fourth in the AL in strike-outs per nine inning (7.04). He also placed seventh in hit-batsmen with eight.

May 15, 1973 was notable for Stone. Former Orioles fly chaser Pat Kelly, then with the White Sox, doubled in a run the 12th inning at Oakland. It gave the Sox a 6-5 lead. But the A's fired back with three singles and threatened to overtake the Sox. Stone was called in from the bullpen to face Joe Rudi and Gene Tenace with the winning run standing at second. He struck out both hitters and earned his first and only Major League save.

A year and 13 days after his first trade experience, Stone was sent packing again. His uniform again would spell Chicago but this time it was the National League club, the Cubs. Lefty Ken Frailing and rookie catcher Steve Swisher would join Stone in Wrigley. Heading to Comiskey was Cubs legend Ron Santo, who approved the trade to the White Sox after becoming the first 10-and-5 player to veto a trade to California.

The 1974 Cubs would finish dead last while dropping 96 games. Stone would make several relief appearances before making his initial start on April 30 at the Astrodome.

Facing future Astros skipper Larry Dierker, Stone went $6\frac{1}{3}$ innings against the Astros, allowing five hits and two earned runs. He actually departed in the seventh with a 2-1 lead, as manager summoned reliever Horacio Pina with one out after Denis Menke touched Stone for a double. Pina allowed an RBI single to Greg Gross to tie the game and eventually allowed the go-ahead runs in the 4-2 Houston victory.

On the last day of June, Stone wasn't as sharp. After retiring the first two Expos to start the day game in Jarry Park, he allowed two singles and a Mike Jorgenson two-run homer. He also surrendered a run-scoring double to Ken Singleton. The former O's star also singled off Stone before the right-hander headed for the showers in the third inning.

"I faced him when I was in Montreal," Singleton said. "I hit a homer off of him. As they say, it was against a gale-house wind and it still went across the street."

Singleton had three hits in the 10-2 romp. Stone's record was 2-2. On July 9, the home run ball gave Stone fits in his battle against the visiting Reds. In an 8-5 loss, Stone surrendered long balls to Joe Morgan, Tony Perez, Cesar Geronimo, Dan Driessen and Johnny Bench in just 2⅓ innings of labor. The good news for the Cubs, all five of these blasts came with no one on base.

"They hit sliders, curves and fastballs," Stone told the *Chicago Tribune*. "They weren't picking on one pitch."

The five-homer outburst would paste Stone on a list that would be familiar to him in the coming seasons. Stone surrendered 19 homers to chalk up ninth place in the National League. He would tie for ninth place with Expos ace Steve Rogers. However, Rogers logged 84 more innings (253 to Stone's169) than Stone did. Stone finished 8-6 with an ERA of 4.14. He would be on the wrong side of the innings-to-hits ratio, allowing 185 hits in those 169 innings of action. The homer plague would follow him to the 1975 campaign, finishing third in the league with 24 round-trippers. His teammate, Ray Burris, would add on to the pile with 25 homers. The Cubbies picked up nine games in the standings and got a dozen wins from Stone in 1975.

On the first of May, Chicago stood at 13-5, and Stone had four of those victories. He was standing at 5-0 when his strong start was derailed.

"I started 5-0 with the Cubs in 1975," Stone said. "And then I hurt my hip and was disabled a bit."

For the first time in his young career his ERA fell below the 4.00 mark (3.95). He also logged more than 200 innings in a season for the first time (214) and finished a respectable 12-8. Stone was third on the club with his 12 wins.

The 1976 Cubs posted the same number of victories (75) as the year before. And they did it without much help from Stone. Arm miseries cut his innings by two-thirds. He didn't appear in the win column until July 6, when he went 6 strong innings to beat the Padres 4 -0.

Stone and Carlton matched up again in 1976. On Aug. 3, Stone was victimized by two four-run innings. Garry Maddox chased him with a third-inning grand slam. Eight earned runs were stapled to his ERA.

Another J.R. Richard- Steve Stone matchup played at the Astrodome on Aug. 17. Stone again was the first to blink and fell to 3-5 in the 8-1 loss. Stone posted a 3-6 mark with an ERA of 4.08 in 1976, and on Nov. 1, he tested the free agent market. Just 23 days later, his former employer on the South Side of Chicago came calling. He would again jump leagues and pitch for the White Sox in 1977.

The White Sox under Bill Veeck's second ownership regime won 90 games. Stone overcame a slow start to run off five straight victories.

On June 10, Stone and the Sox battled Mike Flanagan and the Birds at Memorial Stadium. Doug DeCinces cleared the filled bags with a double, and the Orioles beat Stone 6-1, chasing Stone in the third.

On May 5, 1980, Minnesota first baseman Glenn Adams homered off Stone leading to his third loss of the season. Stone wouldn't lose again for three months. In 1977, Adams' two-run double in the first and grand slam in the second chased Stone early, and Minnesota outlasted the Sox 19-12, dropping Stone to 8-6.

On Aug. 13, Stone beat the the Rangers 6-5 for his career-best 13th win. On Aug. 24, Stone returned to Memorial Stadium and was greeted by 4 hits from Al Bumbry and four more from Rich Dauer as the O's beat Stone and the Sox 10-5.

A once-in-a lifetime occurrence happened Aug. 29 in Cleveland.

A whopping 6,200 fans turned out to see some Indians history. After Stone fanned Indians leadoff man Paul Dade to open the home team's at-bats, the right-hander set his sights on second-sacker Duane Kuiper. This singles hitter was working on quite a streak himself. In his previous 1,382 at-bats, the lefty swinger had never knocked a ball over any fence in the American League. This was the longest active streak of non-dingers in the Major Leagues. Of course that was homer-happy Stone throwing for the Sox.

Kuiper put a charge into one of Stone's pitches.

"At first, I didn't think it would go out," Kuiper said. "One home run is better than none, but any more than one and people start expecting them."

"He's never let me forget it," Stone told *Baseball Digest*. "He brings it up every time we happen to meet. The only home run of his career, and it had to come off me."

Stone was out of sorts at the start of this contest anyway.

"I was told the game was going to start at 8:40 local time," Stone told the *Chicago Tribune*. "And it started 10 minutes early. I couldn't believe it. I need about about 25 minutes and it was just about halfway through when the umpires came out on the field to start the game. I asked for extra time when it was time for me to pitch but all I got was about a minute. I wasn't ready to pitch. I had nothing in the first inning."

Andy Thornton and Bruce Bochte also left the yard in Stone's 10th loss of the season. Despite those blasts, Stone dropped to seventh in the league in homers allowed (25). He was also ninth in wild pitches (10) which was career-high. In addition, he was 10th in earned runs allowed (104). Despite his sporting 15-12 record, Stone's ERA was an unsightly 4.51. He surrendered 228 hits in 207 innings pitched.

The White Sox slumped badly in 1978. Instead of winning 90 games, Chicago went the other way and lost 90 times. It didn't help the Sox' cause to lose eight of nine games to Stone's future employer. Stone stood at 1-1 when he faced the O's on April 28. He certainly had his way with third baseman Doug DeCinces who struck out three times.

Stone took a two-hit shutout to the eighth before Bumbry broke it up with his first homer of the season. Stone didn't get a decision as Eddie Murray hammered a grand slam later in the frame in the O's 6 -4 win. On June 5, Stone moved two games up on the .500 mark by stifling the Indians on three hits. He also walked six but moved to 5-3 with the 2-0 win. It was his first shutout since August of 1976. Stone again walked six on July 24. And again, he survived. He was now 8-7 on the year after this 5-1 victory over the Brewers.

On the first of September, Stone battled Jim Palmer in Baltimore. He made one major mistake, a two-run homer to leadoff hitter Larry Harlow. Stone pitched eight strong innings against the O's but fell 3-0. For being with a club that was 19 games below the .500 mark, Stone's 12-12 mark was a strong showing. He still had a problem sur-rendering runs and allowed one fewer run than he did the year be-fore (103), he jumped from 10th to seventh on the earned runs list. That boosted his ERA to 4.37.

It was time to test the free agent waters again. The 30-year-old hurler had toiled the past six seasons in a Chicago uniform. He ap-peared in 88 National League games with the Cubs and rang up 23 victories. His South Side log was 97 games and 33 wins. At the height of his career, he wasn't all that thrilled about leaving the Windy City.

"I was hoping right to the end that the White Sox could come up with something." Stone told the *Tribune*. "It was a business decision with Bill (Veeck). I can respect him for that. Our relationship will always be a good one. He is the man I feel responsible for my getting the chance to achieve what I did contractually.".

And who could blame Veeck and the Sox? Instead of dishing out the cash for the well-traveled Stone, they could circle the wagons around the youth of the team such as Ross Baumgarten (23 years-old), Steve Trout (20) and Britt Burns (19).

Stone did not leave cold Chicago bitter.

"Nobody else ever had the confidence to give me the ball two years running and say, "You're a starting pitcher. I guess I'm one of the few free agents who loved Chicago. It's the best city for fans on both sides of town. My six years here were a wonderful experience."

The 1978 Sox (71-90) had the exact opposite record of the O's (90-71) and Stone knew he would get a boost in the standings heading East to Baltimore.

"What jumps out at you," Stone told the *Chicago Tribune*. "Is the lineup with four guys who hit more than 20 home runs apiece (Lee May, Singleton, Murray and DeCinces). And do you realize that 13 guys on that club make their homes in the Baltimore area? And most of them are from California."

The 1978 Baltimore Orioles finished in fourth place. Despite winning 90 games, it was the poorest showing in the AL standings during Earl Weaver's heralded 14-year-run. Weaver's legacy includes a first or second- place finish in a full dozen of those special campaigns. In those days, this wise organization didn't sit around and wait for its older players to cash their Social Security checks. General Manager Hank Peters set out to make his club stronger in the pitching department. He secured the services of the Chicago White Sox free agent and 12-game winner Steve Stone. Peters had recalled seeing Stone pitch at much earlier age. Peters was the vice-president of the Cleveland Indians from 1965-1971.

"I went over to watch a college game in Toledo (against Kent State) mainly to watch Thurman Munson play in a doubleheader," Peters said. "Steve Stone happened to pitch one of the games. Hey, I liked this guy. So when I was with the Indians, we drafted him. But he wouldn't sign with us. He went out and played in a Cape Cod league that summer. He went back into the draft. The Giants drafted him. And he did sign with the Giants. So I eventually got my hands on him."

Stone had joined a club that expected to win. A team that moved from St. Louis to Baltimore in 1954. A dozen years later, the Orioles were World Champions.

> *I make them feel confident, and they make me feel safe. And pretty. Of course what I give them lasts a lifetime. What they give me lasts a hundred and forty-two games. Sometimes it seems like a bad trade. But bad trades are a part of baseball. I mean, who can forget Frank Robinson for Milt Pappas, for God's sake?"*
>
> *-- Annie Savoy in "Bull Durham"*

That, of course, doesn't tell the whole story. Both the Cincinnati Reds of the National League and the Baltimore Orioles of the AL finished exactly eight games out of first place in the pennant chase of 1965. All nine regulars in manager Dick Sisler's lineup hit 10 or more homers. Veteran Frank Robinson led the way with 33 down to second sacker Pete Rose who managed 11.

There was much less power in the Orioles lineup. AL Rookie of the Year Curt Blefary led with just 22 round trippers. Brooks Robinson (18) and Boog Powell (17) joined Blefary in double figures. Orioles general manager Lee MacPhail set out to add some pop to this lackluster offense. He was also in a job search for himself. He succeeded on both accounts.

MacPhail picked a poor time to depart the surging Birds but he jumped ship and took over a similar position with the New York Yankees. However before embarking on his next adventure, he tipped off incoming GM Henry Dalton to a potential trade with the Redlegs. Cincinnati was dangling the 1961 NL MVP in Frank Robinson. On the day that baseball pioneer Branch Rickey passed away at age 83, Reds GM Bill DeWitt sent an unhappy Robinson off to Baltimore in exchange for the pitchers Milt Pappas and Jack Baldschun and outfielder Dick Simpson. Pappas was the big catch in the trade having won 13 of his 34 starts and sporting an ERA of 2.65.

Pappas won just one fewer game in his first season in Cincinnati. However his dozen victories didn't take the sting out of one of the most lopsided trades in baseball history. Frank Robinson won the Triple Crown in his first season in Baltimore. It was baseball's first Triple Crown since Mickey Mantle's magical season in New York a decade earlier.

Granted, Robinson's .316 batting average is the poorest in a Triple Crown season, but his power game (49 homers) made up for it. Robinson stayed with the Orioles for six seasons before being dealt back to the National League. In four of those campaigns (1966, 69, 70, 71), the Orioles reached the World Series.

Stone had departed Chicago for a baseball team that knew how to win. Fiery manager Earl Weaver took the head job from Hank Bauer at the All-Star break of 1968. In his nearly 15 seasons, his club never posted a losing season. In 11 of those campaigns, the Birds won 90 or more games. Weaver's record during that stunning run was 1,354-919.

Weaver was also blessed with great talent including Hall-of-Famers Robinson, Brooks Robinson, Jim Palmer, Eddie Murray and Cal Ripken Jr. It's worth focusing in on the run from 1969 through 1971, when Baltimore made three consecutive appearances in the Fall Classic. They managed 317 wins and just 164 losses. Only World Series defeats to the Pirates and Mets could take away from seasons that could only be compared to the Ruthian Yankees campaigns.

Are we likely to see four 20-game winners again? The year was 1971 with Palmer (20) , Mike Cuellar (20) , Dave McNally (24) and Pat Dobson (20).

You couldn't have dreamed up a better campaign than the 1979 season. One more victory would have added to the World Series hardware. The Birds dropped eight of their first 11 games, and then the club positively ignited. Stone picked up his first two Orioles victories during Baltimore's 9-game winning streak. In the first three months of the season, the Birds were scary at Memorial Stadium, winning 30 of 39 contests. The 79 Orioles had baseball's best record (102-57). No other Major League club hit the century mark that season. Both the Brewers and Red Sox won more than 90 games but had nothing to show for it. The Blue Jays finished 50 ½ games behind Baltimore.

Stone did not immediately endear himself to Orioles fans. He would walk seven in his Orioles debut on April 13. The third batter of the night, Cecil Cooper of Milwaukee, took Stone's offering out at County Stadium and he was behind 2-0. The O's lost three men to ejections (Singleton, manager Earl Weaver and coach Cal Ripken, Sr.), and Stone fell in his debut, 9-3. He would meet that same Brewers club exactly a week later in Baltimore. And despite allowing another homer to Cooper and a solo shot to Sixto Lezcano, Stone registered his first O's win, 6-3. Baltimore would win 16 of its next 17 games and surged to an American League pennant.

On June 6, Dennis Martinez beat Kansas City to move to 8-2 on the season. Both Palmer and Flanagan sported 6-2 records. And the free agent Stone was stuck at 3-5. On July 7, Stone surrendered seventh inning homers to former O's Don Baylor and Bobby Grich in a 7-3 loss to the Angels in Anaheim. Stone stood at 6-7 with an ERA of 4.40.

The crowds in Baltimore were not used to mediocrity.

"Every time I picked up a newspaper, I read that I should be banished to the bullpen," Stone said to the *Baltimore Sun*. "There were some unpleasant noises whenever my name was announced. They booed the hell out of me, and that was not a pleasant experience. I wasn't pleased with what was going on."

Ninety games into the 1979 season, the O's had the best mark in the Major Leagues (59-31).

"I was our only weakness," Stone said. "Everybody else was having a Renaissance year. I was like a Chrysler."

Baltimore Sun scribe Ken Nigro penned an article for the *Sporting News* in late July. He, too found much to complain about the new Orioles pitcher.

"Stone clearly has been a major disappointment," Nigro wrote. "No one thought he was going to be another Cy Young when the Orioles signed him to a four-year contract as a free agent last winter. But no one thought he was going to get blown away so often, either."

The positive thinker of 1980 was nothing of the sort in the first half of this season.

"I had all negative thoughts about my pitching, about my environment, about everything," he said. "I realized I had to realign my thinking. I felt it was up to me to make the situation turn around. I was 0-for-3 in arguments with Earl and I knew he wasn't going to change. But I realized that our goal was the same – to win."

Stone did some reflecting during the All-Star break

"It was a period of introspection," Stone recalled 25 years later. "I would meditate before games. I would look at the batters in my mind and get all 27 outs. I would go a couple of hours at it."

It paid dividends. He wouldn't lose the rest of the season. On July 22, he struck out 10 Oakland A's on route to a 4-1 win.

Stone won 11 games for the 1979 AL East Champion Orioles, who won 102 games.. Again, opposing teams figured out ways to punish his mistakes. Stone allowed a career-high 31 home runs. He was fourth in the AL, and as if it were clockwork, every six innings he pitched one ball that would be sent sailing over a fence.

Hall-of-Famer Ferguson Jenkins surrendered 484 taters in his distinguished career. Exactly 40 came in 1979 when he easily claimed the league lead. Jenkins worked 259 innings that summer but allowed just one long ball to a Baltimore Oriole named Kiko Garcia. In second place in this ignominious category was Royals ace Dennis Leonard. He was clearly a distant second with 33 in 236 frames. The Orioles, as a team, had more success against this right-hander delivering 22 homers during his pitching career. That was the most Leonard surrendered to any AL team in his dozen seasons of hurling. Tied for second with Leonard was Brewers southpaw Billy Travers. And this 14-game winner used 49 fewer innings to accomplish this feat. And finally, in third place, came the O's top free agent of 79. In 32 starts, Stone fell just short of a homer a game. In just over 186 innings, Stone broke his own mark of 25 set as a member of the 1977 Chisox.

"I liked to spread the joy around," Stone joked. "I was a high fastball pitcher who threw a curve. And when that curve doesn't break, they go forever. I think I gave up a few in Chicago and the scoreboard would go off. Eddie Murray called me 'Boom Boom' after all that noise. But some of the best pitchers gave up a lot of homers. Ferguson Jenkins gave up a lot of solo homers."

Stone's World Series experience centers on 12 Pittsburgh Pirates hitters he faced on Oct. 13, 1979 in Pittsburgh. The Pirates held a slim 4-3 lead at Three Rivers Stadium entering the home half of the fifth inning. And after two of those dozen hitters, Stone was in immediate trouble. Stone walked shortstop Tim Foli, and slugger Dave Parker lined a hit to left setting the stage for Pops. Eventual 1979 World Series MVP, Willie Stargell stood at the plate and threatened to bust open the fourth game of the series. After all, Stargell homered to open the second inning, an inning in which the Pirates chased starting pitcher Dennis Martinez with four runs. Stargell had also doubled in the third inning.

Against Stone, all Pops could muster was a pop up, which third baseman DeCinces squeezed for the first out. Stone wasn't out of trouble though. John Millner pulled a ball to right field and earned an RBI for his trouble. With the Pirates up 5-3, Stone was told to intentionally walk Billy Madlock to load the sacks. Weaver didn't reach for the hook despite another left-handed bat coming up.

And Stone escaped. Ed Ott flied to Roenicke in left. One ground ball to Garcia at shortstop limited the damage to just one run.

The sixth inning presented Stone with little trouble to start. His first World Series strikeout opened the inning as pitcher Jim Bibby didn't put up much of a struggle. The second out came when Omar Moreno bounced out to Dauer at second. But this was not to be a 1-2-3 frame. Foli reached base again as he dropped a ball into right field. Parker was up next and again went the opposite way with a Stone pitch, with a two-bagger to left to chase Foli home and make it 6-3. Perhaps in disgust, Stone struck out Stargell to end the inning. However, two earned runs in two innings of work spells out an ugly 9.00 ERA. Any disappointment on Stone's part was soon erased by a memorable six-run eighth inning that gave the Orioles a 9-6 win to put them up three games to one. The O's were nine innings away from a World Championship. Of course, history wrote a different ending to this tale.

The O's of 79 won six post-season games but fell one game short of a world championship. The pieces were certainly in place for another run at the glory. With a pitching staff that included future Hall-of Famer Palmer, Dennis Martinez, and southpaws Flanagan and Scott McGregor, there wasn't much room for the average Steve Stone in Weaver's pitching rotation. Stone could read the writing on the wall. This pitching staff was set – yes – in Stone.

"It was the All-Star break of 1979," Stone said. "Earl and I went at it. I told him he was the most disgusting human being I had ever been around and that I wanted to be traded. He said, 'We got you to be our fifth starter, and that's what you will do.'

"He said he was only going with three pitchers in September. It didn't look like I would have a chance. But he didn't go to three. And I had 13 starts after the break and went 5-0."Stone grew to respect the ornery Weaver. Was it just a coincidence that Baltimore had the game's best pitching year-in and year-out?

"Managers have to have a feeling when a pitcher is losing it," Stone said. "I had just hung a curve and some guy hit it about eight miles. It was 100 feet foul. Earl came out. I said. 'Earl it's a foul ball.'

" 'Yes,' Earl said, 'but the next one won't be.' "

May 5, 1980

American League East	W	L	Pct.	GB
New York	12	9	.571	—
Toronto	12	9	.571	—
Milwaukee	10	8	.556	½
Boston	11	10	.524	1
Baltimore	9	12	.429	3
Detroit	8	14	.364	4½
Cleveland	7	13	.350	4½

Pitching Matchup

Minnesota (Pete Redfern 3-1, 1.46) at Baltimore (Steve Stone 2-2, 4.50)

4

Last loss

Rob Wilfong and Glenn Adams didn't exactly scare American League pitchers in the 1980's. Wilfong averaged 3.5 homers a year in his 11-year run on both the Twins and Angels. Adams was little more powerful delivering 4.2 long balls a season during his eight-year career. In 1979, Robert Donald Wilfong of Pasadena, California, led the American League in sacrifices.

Unluckily for Stone, Wilfong couldn't lay down a sacrifice when the left-handed hitter approached the batter's box in the visitor's first at-bats on May 5. That's because leadoff hitter Hosken Powell bounced one to first-sacker Murray.

Wilfong's first-inning homer off of Stone was his fourth round-tripper of the young season, half his season total in only game 24 for the Twins.

Mike Cubbage would bat 30 points lower in 1980 (.246) than the preceding year. That didn't stop the southpaw swinger from reaching

Stone for a two-bagger to open the second. It was clear Stone didn't bring his best stuff out in the early innings.

Rick Sofield would bat 612 times in a Minnesota Twins uniform before finding something else to do with his life. His 141 career whiffs told the story of his short career. Sofield did make contact with a Stone pitch, however, driving it to Bumbry in center for the second out. Cubbage tagged and scored his team's second run. Designated hitter Glenn Adams led off the fourth for the Twins. Naturally batting left-handed, Adams would never bat more that 350 times in one season during his eight-year run as a member of the Giants, Twins and Blue Jays. But he, too, homered off the 1980 Cy Young Award winner. His fourth-inning blast was his initial long ball of the campaign.

It was not the first one Adams hit off Stone during an otherwise pedestrian career. Three years earlier, Adams had a career day at the expense of Stone. He had a two-run double in the first and a grand slam homer in the second on the way to an 8-RBI game in which Stone did not survive the third inning. Of the 184 long balls Stone dealt out in his 1,788 innings l, Adams grand slam was the lone bases -clearing homer he ever surrendered.

(As impressive as that is, his one grand slam is still one more than Baltimore teammate Jim Palmer gave up in more than 2,100 more innings.)

Adams would enter the Twins' record books with 8 RBI in the 19-12 romp.

"That was a fairly good day," Adams said three decades later "My parents came in the day before from Boston so that was nice to see. I knocked those two runs into right field. I pulled most everything in those days. I hit his fastball for the homer. I was hoping it would be over the right fielder's head. I think it might have gone out by two or three feet. It was the best day I ever had."

Teammate Rod Carew drove in six that same day, and his four hits (two off of Stone), pushed his season mark to .403. Adams recalled reporters surrounding Carew after the slugfest on June 26, 1977.

"He told them he wasn't going to talk until they talked to me first," Adams recalled. "I thought that was very generous."

Carew was not on the Twins' club that led Stone and the Orioles 3 -0 early in 1980. In the home half of the fourth, lightning struck literally. After Singleton doubled and Murray singled him home, the rains came. It was a passing shower that caused a rain delay of 11 minutes. It was long enough for the match to go out on the Orioles rally. Stone and the Birds were down 3-1. The aforementioned Wilfong would be in the middle of the next Twins rally in the fifth. In addition to his skills laying down bunts, Wilfong could occasionally swipe a base. Of his 54 career stolen bases in his 11-year run, 39 of those came in his first four years in the bigs. After drawing a one-out walk, Wilfong stole second and later advanced to third when third baseman Rayford butchered a Ken Landreaux grounder. He scored on a Cubbage single, ending Stone's night.

Twins right-hander Pete Redfern was Stone's mound foe this night. The first pick in the 1976 amateur baseball draft, Redfern was tied with Oakland's Mike Norris for the AL lead in strikeouts (33). After fanning four Orioles into the sixth inning, Redfern departed when Crowley's sixth-inning hit plated Murray cutting the Twins' lead in half.

Minnesota reliever Doug Corbett was simply brilliant in 1980. The 27-year-old rookie hurled 136 innings of relief and surrendered just 103 hits. His ERA was 1.98 and he registered eight wins and 23 saves. Corbett relieved Redfern in the sixth and quieted the O's attack.

Baltimore loaded the bases in the ninth but Lee May fanned to end the game and Corbett picked up a save in three-plus innings of work.

On Monday night, May 5, Stone looked destined for another sub-par campaign. His record stood at 2-3. His ERA was an unsightly

4.74. And he also seemed to have no clue on how to beat the team that left D.C. for the Midwest during the John F. Kennedy Administration. His career mark vs. Minnesota after this game was 0-4 with a dismal 8.32 ERA

"I don't know what it is" Stone told the *Sun*. "Maybe it's just chemistry. I can't say it was all those left-handed hitters, because Kansas City and New York throw just as many left-handers and they're much better left-handers."

Stone's loss in Baltimore ended his eight-consecutive win streak at Memorial Stadium. No one knew it at the time but the right-hander would not lose another game until the middle of August. At least the Orioles (9-13) were consistent in the run department. Orioles pitchers had surrendered 94 runs after these 22 games. Orioles hitters had also scored 94 runs.

May 9, 1980

American League East	W	L	Pct.	GB
Toronto	15	9	.625	—
New York	14	9	.609	½
Milwaukee	11	11	.500	3
Boston	12	12	.500	3
Baltimore	11	14	.440	4½
Cleveland	9	14	.391	5½
Detroit	9	16	.360	6½

Pitching Matchup

Baltimore (Steve Stone 2-3, 4.74) at Milwaukee (Jerry Augustine 0-1, 6.17)

5

Streak begins

Stone's 14-game winning streak would begin innocently enough in Milwaukee, the site of perhaps his best outing in an Orioles uniform, a one-hitter before a *Monday Night Baseball* audience in 1979. Stone hoped to even his record at 3-3 on May 9 as he prepared to match wits with Brewers lefty Jerry Augustine. As Stone was set to take the mound, the O's trailed the fourth-place Brewers by a game and a half. More than 34,000 filled County Stadium to watch the slumping defending AL champs and stars Murray and Singleton and the hometown heroes of Paul Molitor, Cecil Cooper and Robin Yount.

The Saturday morning box score showed O's leftfielder Gary Roenicke had just one hit in this 5-2 win. However, his glove saved a couple of runs when the 6-foot-3 glove man stole a two-run homer from Milwaukee's Sixto Lexcano in the home half of the sixth.

"We played good defense behind (Stone)," Roenicke said. "He had some good luck. I know he had some superstitious things. We just knew when he was going out there, we had a good chance to win."

The tying run was on base when Lezcano pumped one high and deep towards left field.

"It was hit so high," Roenicke told the *Milwaukee Journal* that night. "It was too hard to read right away. When he hit it, I ran back to the fence and waited. Anytime you can save a home run, it's a great feeling."

Stone stood incredulously as the ball threatened to leap into the stands.

"I was surprised the ball went as far as it did," Stone said. "I didn't think Lezcano hit it real well."

Baltimore gave Stone a quick 1-0 lead in the first. The pure speed of the Bumble Bee Al Bumbry was clearly behind the tally. Bumbry entered this contest in the top five in the AL in both runs scored and stolen bases. Not bothered by the southpaw Augustine, Bumbry went the opposite way for a single. He would hit a screaming .388 in the month of May and, along with his pitcher on the mound, was especially helpful in pulling the Orioles out of their April doldrums. Bumbry watched Belanger fly harmlessly to center before getting a good read on Augustine. He took off for second and swiped the bag for number nine on the season. He would score an out later on what was scored a pop-up to the second baseman, Jim Gantner.

But two batters into the home half and Stone was already in hot water.

Future Hall-of-Famer Robin Yount jumped a Stone pitch and sent it scurrying past Roenicke in left for a one-out double. The 24-year-old shortstop, who two years later would hit two homers off Jim Palmer in the final game of his 1982 MVP season, would lead the AL with 49 doubles in 1980, which was Yount's first breakout season. Stone managed to get fierce Cecil Cooper out on a fly to center. That was an accomplishment in itself as Cooper led the AL in total bases that season (335). With two outs, Stone threw one past catcher Dempsey. This sent Yount dashing to third and set the tone for the next two hitters. Dick Davis and Don Money each walked to load the bases for Lezcano.

Lezcano, a right-handed hitter, was coming off his best Big League season, an MVP-like 79 campaign. He was third in the AL in slugging percentage (.573) and hit a sharp .321 with career highs in homers (28) and RBI (101). On this gusty May night in Milwaukee, Lezcano picked up a quick pair of RBI with a liner to left to put Stone on the short end after one inning, 2-1. However, Lezcano's clutch hit couldn't save Jerry Augustine. The 27-year-old southpaw made 63 starts in 1977-78. His loss on May 9 would mark his lone start of the 1980 season. And there was a good reason for it.

American League hitters had figured him out. His ERA jumped more than a full run from 1979. He walked more than he fanned.

By the second inning, the Orioles were just being patient. Three consecutive right-handed hitters went the other way against Augustine. Lezcano evidently earned notice for his first-inning hero-ics as it was his duty to field balls in front of him in right. DeCinces singled to right. Lee May found that scenario to his liking and also dropped one in front of the right-fielder. Dempsey had the third con-secutive safety off the lefty, and the Birds had the sacks loaded with no one out.

Dauer's sacrifice fly knotted the game at two, and a Belanger safety to center put the Birds up a run. Augustine was gone by the third inning and relieved by veteran Brewers righty Bill Castro. The 26-year-old Castro would appear in a career-high 56 games in 1980. He would hurl 3⅓ innings in this contest and surrender just one un-earned run. Meanwhile Stone was getting help from the "pitcher's best friend." Molitor lined into a twin killing in the second. In the fourth inning, Milwaukee had two on for Gorman Thomas, destined for 38 homers that summer. The slugger bounced one to DeCinces at third for a 5-4-3 double play. Yount was next in the double play pa-rade. With Charlie Moore on first in the fifth, Yount smacked one down to DeCinces for two rapid outs. Later in this inning, Paul Molitor found himself with new life when Murray dropped a foul ball. With a second chance, Molitor whiffed.

Meanwhile, Castro allowed a one-out double by Dempsey, followed by a Dauer RBI single to make it 4-2 in the sixth. Stone found some two-out trouble in the seventh. Moore and Money took turns taking Stone up the middle.

"They have the type of lineup, it's like the World Series pitching against them because everybody who's up is an excellent hitter," Stone told the *Journal*. "I think if all clubs were as strong offensively as the Brewers, it would be a long season for the pitchers."

In 1980, 6-foot-4 Dave Ford appeared in nearly half of his career games (25 of 51). The Cleveland, Ohio native was brought in to retire Yount. He kept the ball in the infield but DeCinces had no play at any base. The sacks were loaded for Cooper. Tippy Martinez was ready in the bullpen, and Weaver had no trouble lifting the ball from Ford's hands. With Stone's win in the balance, Martinez induced Cooper to bounce harmlessly to Dauer extinguishing the threat.

"I was just glad to get that kind of relief help," Stone said. "I think Tippy didn't throw one curve to Cooper. Cooper was expecting a breaking ball and he just threw fastballs. That was the pitch of the night."

Dick Davis opened the Brewers eighth with a two-bagger to left. Stoddard was called in to retire Money. He couldn't. The veteran of 13 big league campaigns, Money was seeing his playing time slowly phased out. For the first time since the 1969 season, he batted fewer than 300 times. Money came through, however, chasing Davis to third with a single. Stoddard then resorted to his glovework to secure an out. He snared a Lezcano grounder and threw home to nail Davis. Gantner then pushed one to Belanger and was erased on the fourth twin killing of the night.

"Double plays help everybody," Belanger said to the *Journal*. "For some reason, Stone puts guys on the bases. When you have more runners, you have more chances for double plays. Double plays look a lot bigger when you put a lot of guys on base. Sure, it makes a difference for a pitcher to have good fielders."

Stone was asked about the obvious advantages of playing for a stingy defensive unit. "We had a fine offensive team in Chicago," Stone said of the '77 White Sox, the Southside Hit Men. "But there was nobody who could catch the ball. The Orioles always seem to make the big play, the plays that you have to have."

Stone had seen firsthand the slick fielding of Don Kessinger who had scooped up balls behind him for both Chicago teams. But watching Belanger every day was something different.

"One of the most amazing shortstops I had seen," Stone told *Baseball Prospectus Radio*. "He never dove for the ball. He was magnificent. He hit everybody's fastball. He killed Nolan Ryan. He had a lot of talent; very stubborn. Blade was quite an infielder."

Belanger's second single of the night plated the game's final tally. The O's had lived through 3 Moore singles (no runs scored) and two hits and 2 RBI from Lezcano.

"It really gets down to getting your breaking pitches over the plate," Stone added. "If I don't, they give me lots of trouble. I can remember giving up nine runs in this park. Tonight, I got my breaking pitch over. If you go 2-0, 3-0 all the time, you are not going to last long against this club. If you can't get the breaking ball over, you have to come in with a fastball. They're as good a fastball hitters as there are."

Stoddard earned his 5th save of the season in this contest. Big Foot had all the saves in Stone's three-win collection..

"It's the 'Steve and Tim Show,' " Stone said to the *Sporting News*. "At least I'm making it easy on him. Tim used to come in and get three outs. Then, two and now one out."

Pitching coach Ray Miller was focusing in on a different Stone from the year before.

"I think Steve is really into the Oriole thing," Miller told the *Sporting News*. "He stays ahead on the count. He goes right at hitters and realizes we are going to play good defense behind him. I think last year he was trying to compete with everyone rather than just pitch his game."

On May 12, the unthinkable occurred. Texas lefty Jon Matlack beat the Birds, 5-1, pushing the defending American League champions to the basement.

May 13, 1980

American League East	W	L	Pct.	GB
New York	16	11	.593	—
Toronto	15	11	.577	½
Milwaukee	13	12	.520	2
Boston	13	15	.464	3½
Detroit	12	16	.526	4½
Cleveland	11	15	.423	4½
Baltimore	12	17	.414	5

Pitching Matchup

Texas (Ferguson Jenkins 2-2, 4.15) at Baltimore (Steve Stone 3-3, 4.31)

6

Dan Graham grand slam

Daniel Jay Graham fell one safety short of 100 career hits in his three Major League seasons. The 6-foot-1, 205-pound southpaw swinger batted exactly 4 times in a Minnesota Twins uniform in 1979. On Pearl Harbor day that winter, the Twins swapped third baseman Graham to the O's for a first baseman named Tom Chism, another left-handed hitter who had similar success as Graham had as a Twin in 1979. He was 0-for-3.

Chism would never again bat in a Major League game. Graham brought with him an ability to play more than one position and a resume that boasted of a California League MVP award in 1976. Playing for Reno, he hit a robust .320 with a league-leading 29 homers and 115 RBI. The slugger also struck out 121 times. In 1981, his last year in an Orioles uniform, he barely registered with a tragic .176 average in 142 plate appearances.

Steve Stone's greatest season was also Dan Graham's Major League zenith. The 25-year-old would get 74 percent of his career hits in this campaign. Graham would score 82 percent of his career runs, obtain 70 percent of his doubles, hit his only career triple, belt 88 percent of his homers and collect 83 percent of his RBI. He was especially effective with his lumber when Stone took the mound. In games where he caught Stone, Graham ranked third on the team in RBI (16) to Murray and Singleton, despite getting 80 fewer at-bats. A full third of his 15 homers transpired in Stone contests. Almost 30 percent of his RBI benefited No. 32 in Baltimore's rotation.

On this hot and humid Tuesday night in Baltimore, fewer than 13,000 turned out to see the Texas Rangers, who were formerly the second incarnation of the Washington Senators. This was despite the presence of seven-time 20-game winner Ferguson Jenkins. Six of those splendid seasons came in a Chicago Cubs uniform.

In 1974, he broke into the 25-victory club in first season in Texas. Stone wasn't ducking the future Hall-of-Famer Jenkins or the oppressive heat.

"When I woke up this morning and heard it was going to be 90 degrees, I was ecstatic," Stone told the *Sun* that day. "That's the best thing that happened all year."

Graham was fresh off the Rochester farm club and would make an immediate impression. He would single to right in the second inning. After fanning in the fourth, he drilled his first Major League homer in the sixth. In the eighth, Jenkins was gone.

Reliever Jim Kern was asked to retire the rookie with two on and two out. The 31-year-old Kern was one of the top relievers in baseball in 1979 with a 13-5 record and a splendid 1.57 ERA. He was second in the AL in saves (29) and fourth in the Cy Young Award voting behind the O's Mike Flanagan. He also logged 143 innings without making a single start. It obviously took its toll. By 1980, he pitched in half as many games and posted an abysmal 3-11 mark.

Graham ripped a single to left-center chasing both Kelly and Murray with the go-ahead runs but pinning the 4-2 loss on Jenkins. There was plenty of praise for the hitting hero of this game.

"If he stays around awhile, I don't think anyone will be saying they shouldn't get beat by a Dan Graham," said Rangers catcher Jim Sundberg. "He's strong, real strong. He impressed me when we saw him in spring training and again now."

Sundberg admitted to the *Dallas Morning News* that young Graham did hit mistakes.

"The home run was a changeup over the middle of the plate," he said. "And when he singled off of Kern, it was a fastball over the plate again."

The Orioles must have known something was afoot as backup catcher Dave Skaggs was sold to the Angels on this same day.

The Texas Rangers of May 12 were in the hunt in the AL West. They were three games over .500 and stood just a game and a half behind first-place Oakland. When the season concluded, Texas did not have one 20-homer hitter in the lineup. Of course, Al Oliver's 19 homers and career-high 42 doubles helped drive in a whopping 117 runs.

Catcher Sundberg led off the third inning by taking Stone out of the yard to tie the game at one. Three different times in his solid career this backstop would notch exactly 10 homers. In the middle of May, this was already his fifth homer of the campaign.

In the fourth, Oliver was pained twice. First, Stone hit him with a pitch to open the inning. Then, the new star, Graham, caught him stealing for the first out of the inning, adding insult to his mild injury. That was especially important because one out later, Pat Putnam singled. The Rangers didn't wait around the next time up. Mickey Rivers was a season removed from his glory years in Yankees pinstripes. However, he would notch career-highs in doubles (32) and hits (210) during the 1980 campaign. Rivers' two-bagger chased home the go ahead run, Pepe Frias, who was in the middle of his lone season with Texas following his six-year run in Montreal.

Stone did not allow a Rangers hit in the next three innings. His routine fly ball pitch was especially effective in the visitor's sixth. Clean-up hitter Buddy Bell hit a career-high .329 in 1980, and opened the frame with a fly-out to Pat Kelly in left. Pat Putnam pulled one in the air to right field and Singleton snagged for out No. 2. The equal-opportunity pitcher then induced Richie Zisk to pop one up to Bumbry in center for the final out.

The loser Jenkins was still fuming after this loss. He wanted to take back that change-up he threw to Graham. He was asked what he should have thrown instead.

"I should have thrown up," Jenkins quipped.

While Jenkins and Sundberg confused each other, Stone and Graham seemed like old friends after their first engagement.

"I worked well with Dan and I thought he caught a real fine game," Stone said. "He stayed with the ball and did a terrific job."

With a two-run cushion in the ninth inning, Stone went for the complete game. First baseman Pat Putnam flied to right for the first out. But Richie Zisk reached safely and Weaver had seen enough. In came Stoddard and down went pinch-hitter Danny Walton on strikes. Yes, that Danny Walton who had one eye-opening season in a Brewers lineup one decade earlier, turning in a 17-homer, 20-double campaign. That was 17 of his career 28 homers and 20 of 27 doubles. Less than three weeks after his encounter with Stoddard in 1980, Walton was out of the big leagues forever.

Stoddard closed the game getting Sundberg to bounce to late-inning defensive replacement Mark Belanger.

Stone felt this was one contest that he could have tossed a complete game.

"If ever I was going to finish a game, I thought it would be this one," Stone said.

No. 32 in a Birds uniform was beginning to make a statement. Stone's victory had pulled the Birds within four games of first.

Despite Stone's fourth win, the Orioles would lose two of three to Texas and then head to Detroit. On May 19, the Birds (15-19) began a four-game series with the Cleveland Indians. Stone was matched against the tall left-hander and workhorse of the Tribe staff, Rick Waits. This intriguing matchup played in front of more than 73,000 empty seats in Cleveland.

On June 5, 1978, these two pitchers also met up in front of 108 fewer spectators. Stone, hurling for the White Sox, allowed two hits to leadoff hitter Paul Dade and one to Buddy Bell. That was it in a three-hit complete game shutout. Entering this contest, he had not thrown a 9-inning shutout since that victory..

Less than two years later, Waits was tied for the AL lead in losses (five) just one year after winning a career-high 16 games for Cleveland. The Indians were a last-place team and had only Mike Hargrove's decent on-base percentage to brag about. The future Orioles manager was tied for the AL lead in hit by pitch (four).

In the home half of the first inning, Hargrove helped his future employers by grounding a Stone pitch the opposite way to Dauer who got two outs on the one pitch, turning the double play.

For Waits' part, he kept the ball in play. He surrendered no extra base hits in his 5 + innings of work. Of course there was that matter of three Dempsey singles, two one-base hits each off the bat of Murray, Singleton and Bumbry. DeCinces, May and Garcia also had singles off of Waits during his spell on the mound. In the fifth, the O's grew weary of leaving all those runners stranded. Murray broke for second and fooled Waits. In the meantime, Roenicke broke home and both runners earned stolen bases when the Indians lefty blinked.

May then went the opposite way with a single also in the fifth making it 3-0 Birds. In the early innings, Stone had his strikeout pitch working. He struck out veteran designated hitter Cliff Johnson, leading off the second. An out later, he made third-sacker Toby Harrah look at a called third strike.

Harrah would score exactly 100 runs in 1980, but he fanned twice and bounced to third in his night against Stone. Dempsey's third hit chased Waits and drove in the game's fourth run in the sixth. Lefty reliever Sid Monge was also coming off his best campaign in 1979. He would earn a career-high 12 victories during his 76 appearances that season. He wasn't the same pitcher a year later but allowed just one Singleton single heading to the ninth inning. From the fifth to the ninth, Stone surrendered just one hit. Leadoff batter Miguel Dilone raised his batting average 121 points from the year before. He would finish third in the league in hitting (.341) and third in stolen bases (61). He would be the lone Indian with more than one hit in this contest. The switch-hitter led off the home half of the ninth inning by pulling a ball to right field. One out later,Hargrove pulled a ball to left. Stone induced Johnson to pop the ball in the air to left fielder Roenicke, bringing him an out away from that complete game shutout. Up stepped 27-year-old catcher Ron Hassey. Eight years later he would double and homer while hitting .500 in Oakland's four-game sweep of Boston in the ALCS. He was up for the task on this night also. Stone's shutout was ruined when Hassey dropped one in front of Singleton in right chasing home the fleet-footed Dilone. Even with the two whiffs of Harrah on his record, Weaver took no chances and reached for a fresh arm, Stoddard. Harrah bounced to DeCinces and the contest was over, 4-1.

"I had better stuff in my last start," Stone said. "And I think that might have been because I've had six days off. But my location was excellent. I don't think I missed a spot all night. I want to pitch a complete game before my career ends."

Still, Stone allowed just six singles to the Indians. One of those safeties came off the bat of second baseman Duane Kuiper. Yes, the same Duane Kuiper who hit exactly one career homer in his 3379 Major League at-bats. It came in 1977 vs. White Sox righty Steve Stone.

"I know he gave up Duane Kuiper's only Major League homer," Singleton said. "He almost gave up another one to him as well.''

In his third consecutive victory, Stone walked just one and fanned six. His pitching record suddenly looked respectable at 5-3. And better yet, this victory marked the first time since May of 1971 that the right-hander had posted a career mark more than .500. After seven decisions in a Giants uniform, Stone stood at 4-3. Now after this victory, his career mark stood at 83-82.

1980 AL Cy Young Candidates

1979 Statistics

Player	W	L	S	ERA	G	IP	H	BB	SO
Mike Norris (OAK)	5	8	0	4.80	29	146⅓	146	94	96
Tommy John (NY)	21	9	0	2.96	37	276⅓	268	65	111
Larry Gura (KC)	13	12	0	4.47	39	233⅔	226	73	85
Goose Gossage (NY)	5	3	18	2.62	36	58⅓	48	19	41
Dan Quisenberry (KC)	3	2	5	3.15	32	40	42	7	13
Steve Stone (Bal)	11	7	0	3.77	32	186	173	73	96

Career Statistics (through 1979)

Player	W	L	S	ERA	G	IP	H	BB	SO
Mike Norris (5 seasons)	12	25	0	4.67	87	385⅓	366	224	216
Tommy John (16 seasons)	192	142	4	2.99	487	3082⅓	2919	862	1722
Larry Gura (10 seasons)	56	37	13	3.49	234	949⅔	922	272	395
Goose Gossage (8 seasons)	55	59	101	3.14	359	910⅓	747	415	733
Dan Quisenberry (1 season)	3	2	5	3.15	32	40	42	7	13
Steve Stone (1 season)	78	79	1	4.06	268	1475	1420	588	886

7

The Contenders

Despite winning a Major League high 25 games, Stone was not a runaway choice as Cy Young Award winner. That was no knock on the new Baltimore ace but rather a tribute to the competition. By age 25, Mike Norris had logged five underwhelming seasons in an Oakland uniform. He had seven complete games and a 13-25 record to show for it. As Norris explained during his special 1980 season, he wasn't mature enough to handle success.

"I overindulged in every thing," Norris said in the *Newark Star-Ledger*. "I figured life was one party. I drank too much. I partied too much and thought seriously too little."

When his 22-win season concluded, Reggie Jackson, then with the Yankees, was one of his biggest supporters.

"Norris is the best pitcher in the league," Jackson said. "But he's pitching in Oakland so nobody knows about him. "

Naturally, the Yankees presented a few candidates in the Cy Young Award contest. Southpaw Tommy John was no one-year fluke.

Despite a great career, his legacy will always be that surgery that bears his name. In 1974, Dr. Frank Jobe declared a 100-to-1 shot of repairing Los Angeles Dodgers lefthander John's elbow. Nowadays, Tommy John surgery is common place surgery. Back then, the procedure of replacing the ulnar collateral ligament with a part of a tendon from the non-throwing wrist was nothing short of miraculous. After spending 15 months working his way back, John would post three 20-win seasons. The joke from John goes like this: As he asked Jobe for a Sandy Koufax fastball, he instead received a Mrs. Sandy Koufax speed ball. John relied on a sinkerball and threw the ball at batter's knees. Unlike Stone, he didn't surrender long balls. In 265 innings of action in 1980, John allowed just 13 homers. This was one experienced pitcher who was given a second chance.

"Patience," John told the *New York Times*. "That's what an older pitcher has that a younger pitcher doesn't. When you're younger, you challenge a hitter and you'll get beat. But when I'm 3-0 or 3-1 on a hitter, I know a walk is better than giving him a fat pitch. The only trouble is when you're old, other people sometimes tend to lose patience with you quickly."

John's teammate, fireballer and closer Rich Gossage, could be added to the list of Cy Young contestants. Gossage didn't mess around. He fired bullets at opposing hitters, daring them to hit it. Gossage made 29 starts for the 1976 White Sox and never started a game the rest of his professional career. Instead, he substituted 280 saves in a career that closed 14 years later in Seattle and eventually landed him in the Hall of Fame.

The American League champion Kansas City Royals also had a southpaw of note. Larry Gura would have the first of his two 18-win seasons. His closer, 27-year-old Dan Quisenberry, had his breakthrough season in just his second Big League campaign, piling up 33 saves for the Royals.

As grueling as the Cy Young race was, the American League East was even more competitive. It had been the case for most of the previous 11 seasons of divisional play.

General George Steinbrenner wasn't going to put up with it . There may have been rejoicing in Baltimore after the 102 victories in 1979, but 89 wins and fourth place wouldn't play in New York. Steinbrenner's love-hate relationship with manager Billy Martin had officially closed for the first time. Low-key Dick Howser would take the reins in 1980. The first task was the to find a capable replacement for the fallen Yankees captain. Thurman Munson scored a run on the night of Aug. 1, 1979 at Chicago's Comiskey Park. He never played another game for the Bronx Bombers. Munson died in a plane crash the next day in Canton, Ohio, on an off day.

In addition to being a star for the Yankees, Munson attended Kent State University with Steve Stone. As the right-hander was in the shadow of the great Orioles pitchers, that same feeling took hold in college ball as well.

Munson was the star of Stone's Kent State team.

It wasn't until Stone's broadcasting career in Chicago did it fully hit him what this loss meant to New York and to all of baseball. He passed through the Yankees locker room and saw Munson's locker still sitting open at the end of a row.

"It set chills up my spine," Stone told *Baseball Prospectus Radio*. "Thurman probably would have been in the Hall of Fame."

The battery from Kent State produced one Cy Young Award winner and one MVP.

"He was my catcher," Stone said. "He went to the Yankees for a sizable bonus. I went to the Giants as an afterthought."

Munson was the man in Ohio. He could do it all.

"Ohio is a big state," Stone said. "There are a lot of high schools. Thurman was All-State in baseball, basketball and football."

Stone also recalled how the sophomore catcher picked off eight straight runners off of third base.

"He was a unique character," he said. "He thought he could win at everything; that was the way he lived his whole life. Unfortunately, he probably bit off a little more than he could chew. He crashed in Canton. He was great; he could have been greater."

On Oct. 17, 1979, O's second sacker Rich Dauer led off the third inning with a homer off Pittsburgh pitcher Jim Bibby. It gave the O's a 1-0 lead with 18 outs to go before claiming their third World Championship. The lead didn't hold up as the Pirates won the 1979 Series, four games to three.

Thirteen days later, Steinbrenner began to rebuild his club for the following season and beyond. First sacker Chris Chambliss, infielder Damaso Garcia and pitcher Paul Mirabella went north of the border in exchange for Toronto left-hander Tom Underwood and catcher Rick Cerone. Underwood would feature prominently in the Stone saga as he was the sacrificial lamb in three of Stone's victories. Cerone would drive in a career-high 85 runs for the 1980 Yankees, and he would figure into the American League Most Valuable Player voting.

The wheeling and dealing wasn't done on Nov. 1 when New York set its sights on the other expansion team, Seattle. The target was perhaps the Mariners' best player in outfielder Rupert Jones. The 24-year-old left-handed hitting outfielder had played in all 162 contests and scored 109 runs. He would never get close to those numbers again in his dozen years in a Major League uniform.

That same Thursday, Boston slugger Bob Watson applied for free agency. And a week later, he opted for Yankees pinstripes. Watson, Jones, Cerone, and Underwood were now Yankees. The Orioles would have to counter. Versatile Lenn Sakata came from Milwaukee in exchange for minor league pitcher John Flinn. In another deal that was hardly earth-shattering, AAA players Tom Chism and Dan Graham were swapped. The Orioles did get some mileage out of this deal when Graham's bat started cooking in May.

The Red Sox did better in the free agent market with the addition of Stone-killer Tony Perez. But the former Expo was turning 37, so maybe it wouldn't affect the AL East race that much.

On the last day of May, two clubs in baseball had 28 wins. The Dodgers (28-18) held two-game leads over both the Astros and Reds in the National League West. And the Yankees (28-16) had surged to a 4 ½-game advantage over the Brew-Crew. The O's were mired in fifth place, 7 games back.

While Stone rested, the Cy Young race unexpectedly tightened. That's because both of his main contenders dropped decisions on May 20. John suffered his first loss in Detroit this night. Graig Nettles and Willie Randolph each cracked homers to stake John to a 5-1 lead entering the home half of the fifth. And then it turned ugly for the visitors. Richie Hebner would crack a pair of homers in Detroit's 12-8 win. John did not have a friend calling balls and strikes.

"You could see he was upset," said Yankees catcher Rick Cerone in the next day's *New York Times*. "He was upset with the calls from the first inning."

John had remarkably pitched 110⅓ innings without surrendering a homer dating back to 1979.

Oakland's Norris was not having similar problems. He was scattering four hits versus the Royals. Norris allowed only one run in eight innings. Unfortunately for him, his teammates couldn't touch winless Rich Gale. The A's hard-luck right-hander would drop to 5-2 after this painful 1-0 loss. On this date, Norris still led the entire major leagues in ERA with a 0.52 mark. Ironically, Gale entered this contest with the worst ERA in the majors (6.89).

May 23, 1980

American League East	W	L	Pct.	GB
New York	22	14	.611	—
Toronto	19	16	.577	2½
Boston	19	18	.514	3½
Milwaukee	16	18	.471	5
Detroit	16	20	.444	6
Baltimore	17	21	.447	6
Cleveland	15	20	.429	6½

Pitching Matchup

Detroit (Jack Morris 4-4, 4.73) at Baltimore (Steve Stone 5-3, 3.35)

8

Bumble Bee

Stone was scheduled the next night in a matchup with Detroit's Jack Morris.

Scheduled was the key word here. At approximately 5 a.m., players and owners averted a baseball strike. A four-year basic agreement was announced. Of course, baseball fans would learn how much good this treaty was the following season. Officially 713 baseball games drowned in the summer of 1981.

The Morris-Stone matchup of Friday night, May 23, featured two pitchers traveling in clearly different directions. By the end of the 1980 season, Stone had chalked up 103 of his 107 career victories. The 25-year-old Morris ended 1980 with just 37 of his career 254 wins in the book. Still, the hard-thrower at the top of Sparky Anderson's rotation ate up 250 innings that season. On this night, the two pitchers dominated action. Murray, Graham, DeCinces, Kelly, Roenicke and Belanger united to go 0-for-19. Stone opened the contest by walking the young speedster Kirk Gibson. That in itself was not easy to do. The impatient 23-year-old would accept just 10 free passes in his 175 trips to the plate in 1980. Nothing came of this as Steve Kemp bounced into a twin killing to close the visitor's first inning.

Since breaking into the Majors in a big way in 1973 as Rookie of the Year, Alonza Benjamin Bumbry had been a dazzling leadoff hitter. However, only twice following his rookie campaign did the southern Virginia native bat more than 500 times in a season going into 1980.

The 1980 season was the best campaign of his 14-year career. He set personal marks in games (160), at-bats (645), runs (118), hits (205), homers (9), RBI (53), steals (44), walks (78) and total bases (279). He made his lone appearance on the All-Star team and finished in the top 10 in the AL in every category but doubles, homers and RBI. He also managed to ring up nine triples. In games started by Stone, Bumbry hit a team-high .377 (51-for-135). He also hit four of his nine homers when Stone was pitching. Bumbry was another key player in the miracle year of Steve Stone.

"It was an unlikely event in that he had never won that many ballgames before," Bumbry said. "There aren't that many guys who win that many games in a season. He deserved the All-Star game. It was one of those unusual years."

Bumbry greeted Morris with a bunt base hit. He tested both Morris and catcher Lance Parrish and swiped one of his 44 bases. Dauer and Singleton followed with walks, loading the bases for Murray. Batting left-handed, Murray slapped one the other way but left-fielder Tim Corcoran swallowed it for the first out, although Bumbry raced home on the sacrifice fly. The O's would settle for one run. It was 2-0 in the fifth and Stone was breezing.

The Tigers sixth inning produced the go-ahead runs on one of Murray's nine infield errors of this campaign. He simply misfired on a toss to second base. Stone was hardly ruffled as he began another streak. Eight more Tigers returned to the dugout, but he was in line for his fourth loss trailing by a run with six Oriole outs to go. Two batters later, Stone was off the hook. Bumbry doubled the other way and Dauer singled him home with the tying run. Morris departed but not without some disappointment at being lifted.

"I thought I was pitching well enough to stay in there," Morris said to the *Detroit Free Press*. "I didn't think there was any reason to take me out. I did everything I could and (Anderson) took me out. That's the way the game goes, I guess."

Dave Rozema checked in. The 6-foot-4 right-hander won 15 games as a Houston Astros rookie in 1977. In 1980, he was seventh in the league in wild pitches. Maybe because of that, he was too cautious as Singleton greeted the 23-year-old with a two-run homer, a 400-foot blast to the opposite field, his seventh long ball of the season. The call to the bullpen was made for O's game-closing lefty Tippy Martinez. And he faced nothing but lefties. Hebner struck out sandwiched in between two infield bouncers to Dauer, and Stone's sixth victory was in the books.

No. 32 in the Orioles uniform was beginning to assert himself. Heck, he was chalking up wins like his baseball idol did 15 years ago.

"Being Jewish, I always worshipped Sandy Koufax," he said. "So I took his number (32). Some friends of mine suggested I read Koufax's autobiography. In it, he talked about the philosophy of pitching about how important it was to get ahead of the hitters. Opposing batters had a .119 average off of him when he got ahead in the count, 1-2."

Stone took the mound on Tuesday May 27. His fifth consecutive victory looked to be in the bag early. With Bumbry and Dauer on the bags in the opening frame, 35-year-old Pat Kelly reached right-hander Dan Spillner for a three-run homer into the bullpen in right. Kelly was in his last year as an Oriole. Third baseman Dan Graham must have liked what he saw from Spillner and he, too, went yard providing Stone with a four-run cushion. But this was a night when Stone's magical curve ball wasn't breaking. He wasn't throwing strikes (seven walks) and what went over the plate left in a hurry. Joe Charboneau, on his way to winning the Rookie of the Year award, banged a two-run homer off of Stone in the second inning.

"This was a night when the ball just jumped off the bat," Charboneau said in the next day's *Cleveland Plain Dealer*. "It was fun."

Murray's error at first opened the fatal sixth inning. Rick Manning followed with a two-bagger to right. Mike Hargrove, known as the Human Rain Delay, strolled to the plate.

Ever the patient hitter, (twice led the AL in walks), Hargrove hammered a three-run homer knotting the contest up at 5-5. Jorge Orta walked and so did Stone. He slowly headed to the dugout after being lifted. But there were no reports of the right-hander kicking chairs in the the locker room. The veteran had learned that lesson before.

"I used to have trouble with my temper," he said. "But I learned my lesson pitching for Amarillo, Texas in 1970. I'd just gotten married and I had three bad starts in a row. In the next game, I was leading 1-0 in the fourth inning when the manager yanked me. I was so mad. I went charging into the clubhouse and I saw this plastic trashcan in the middle of the room. I lined it up and figured I'd kick it and hit this clock on the wall. But that can must have had 50 pounds of trash in it and I had shin splints for two weeks. That made me retire from active can-kicking.

"Later that same year, I was going after my 10th win in a game at Shreveport. Well, it had rained real hard the night before and the ballpark there had more leaks than a rusty tub. This time, I got yanked with two out in the eighth and a two-run lead. A left-handed hitter. I had no trouble with was coming up but they brought in a left -hander and the guy doubles up the gap to score three runs and we end up losing. Now, I'm so mad, I'm blind with rage. I forgot about taking the dry route to the clubhouse. I threw my glove in the walkway behind the dugout where there was about three feet of water. Now, I've got to go searching for it through all that muck and sewage.

By the time I find it, my uniform is dripping wet and I've got to wear the damn thing the rest of the road trip, smelling like a sewer rat. Let's just say my temper dissipated after that last incident. What's the sense of carrying on about a loss?

"It's counterproductive. And I'm not the type pitcher who can afford to lose his concentration on the mound. I'm not going to overpower anyone. Get mad and I just might throw the wrong pitch."

Cleveland native Dave Ford was saddled with loss in the 7-6 Indians victory. The 23rd loss of the season did sit well with manager Weaver.

"We've got talent as good as anyone in baseball," Weaver told the *Sun*. "But we're just not getting the job done. Something's just missing somewhere."

Even the reliable Stoddard was touched up in this loss.

"Stoddard can throw a fastball through a car wash without getting it wet," Weaver had once noted.

The bullpen took a share of the blame for this loss.

"We don't have the killer instinct," Weaver barked to the *Plain Dealer*. "Our relief pitchers are awful. If these guys can't do it, we'll get some new ones."

June 2, 1980

American League East	W	L	Pct.	GB
New York	29	16	.644	—
Milwaukee	24	20	.545	4½
Toronto	22	22	.500	6½
Boston	22	24	.478	7½
Baltimore	22	24	.478	7½
Cleveland	21	24	.467	8
Detroit	19	25	.432	9½

Pitching Matchup

Milwaukee (Bill Travers 3-2, 2.90) at Baltimore (Steve Stone 6-3, 3.52)

9

A boost in June

That club in Dauer's hand was still smoking when the Birds welcomed the month of June with the equally hot Milwaukee Brewers coming to town. Boston had felt the power of the Brewers' bats on May's last day. Milwaukee posted an eight-run third inning on the way to a 19-8 victory in the daylight. The visitors produced eight doubles and a pair of homers in the romp. There was more to come the next day. While the O's flew home from Minnesota on June 1, Boston's Steve Renko took a 5-0 lead over the Brewers to the fifth inning. That's when a blister developed as Renko departed seemingly with the game in his pocket.

Jim Dwyer, who would later become an Oriole for five seaons and homer in Game One of the 1983 World Series, had a nightmare of a game at Fenway, however. Dwyer made three errors in 65 games in 1980. All three came in the eight-run seventh inning of this debacle for the Red Sox. The Brewers flew happily to Baltimore after this 8-5 come-from-behind win.

Dauer, who would bat a ringing .352 in Stone outings, was ready for Milwaukee's lefty Bill Travers on this Monday night. However, his evening didn't begin all that well with a throwing error in the opening frame. However, Stone induced veteran Sal Bando to line into a twin killing that lifted Dauer off the hook. The second-sacker responded with his bat, producing singles in the third , fourth, seventh, eighth and 10th innings.

"First of all, he was playing on a very good team," Dauer said of Stone. "It was a very good defensive team. He was a good pitcher who threw a lot of strikes. We did score quite often with him."

A four-run fourth inning gave Stone some breathing room. It could have been a five-run frame if the not-so-swift Dauer hadn't been tossed out trying to score by right-fielder Ben Ogilvie.

The tally would have come in handy on this night. Stone couldn't figure out how to stop fearsome Cecil Cooper. The 6-foot-2 Texan was a good player for part of six seasons in a Red Sox uniform. But the trade of Bernie Carbo and George "Boomer" Scott to Boston in December of 1976 brought over one of baseball's best hitters for nearly a decade. Cooper rarely walked and seldom struck out. He just savagely attacked approaching baseballs. In the top of the fourth, Yount doubled to left field. Cooper chased him home with his fifth homer of the campaign. Stone met Cooper again one inning later. This time, the O's right-hander had a two-run lead. Charlie Moore stood on first base with two outs. Cooper unloaded again and the game was tied at 4-4.

Ben Ogilvie, the American League's leader in homers at this point in June, stepped up to lead off the sixth inning. The man who whipped through New York Times crossword puzzles in minutes also went yard. It was Ogilvie's 13th homer on the way to a career-high 41. Oglivie still had the good manners to compliment the man on the mound.

"It seems like he has more confidence in his pitches. " Ogilvie told *The New York Times*. "He's been very impressive this year."

Ogilvie was the last batter Stone faced on this night. He departed with five earned runs and nine hits on his record. He also moved up on the AL's list of most homers allowed. The blast by Ogilvie gave Stone 11 gopher balls on the campaign and tied him with teammate Flanagan for second-place in the American League. Kansas City's Dennis Leonard held a two-homer advantage.

Neither Dave Ford nor Dennis Martinez was effective in relief. Stoddard hurled an uncharacteristic three full innings of relief. Tippy Martinez earned the win in the 11th inning when former Brewer Lenn Sakata hit his lone homer of the season.

"We scored a lot of runs for him," Sakata said "He never lost and he always wanted to wear the orange top because it was lucky for him. It was just a phenomenal season. A no-brainer season. I think it happens if you have the opportunity to play long enough. Everyone has it in them at the Major League level."

In the 9-8 win, Benny Ayala had his lone triple of the season in a pinch-hitting role. It came in the home half of the eighth inning to tie the contest, and in the process took Stone off the hook in this one.

"It seemed every time he pitched, we were in a groove," Ayala said from his home in Puerto Rico.

With this sudden-death victory, the O's had climbed into a third-place tie with Boston and Toronto.

After 49 games, the Birds were three games below .500, eight games behind the Yankees in the loss column, and one stinking half-game above last-place Detroit. Thegood news was the West Coast trip was scheduled for the weekend. And the Orioles loved playing West Coast teams.

When the 100-win campaign of 1980 had concluded, the Orioles had collected 23 percent of those victories against the Angels, Mariners and Athletics. California was no match for Stone and his comrades. The two teams that met to decide the 1979 American League pennant went in different directions. The Angels dropped 23 games from the year before and slipped out of sight to sixth place. Baltimore took 10 of 12 games in the season series and soared to a lifetime mark of 158-126. Seattle posted the worst record in the AL in 1980 (59-103). If the Birds had taken 10 of 12 vs. Seattle, Stone and his teammates would have repeated as division champions. Instead, the O's and Mariners split the season series at six games each. Despite the glory years of Reggie Jackson and Catfish Hunter, Baltimore dominated the A's in those days. By taking 7 of 12 games this season, the O's overall regular season mark against Oakland swelled to 251-184.

The Cy Young race saw movement on Friday. In Oakland, six-game winner Norris had nothing vs. Boston and was chased in the fifth inning. Future Orioles infielder, Rick Burleson, singled, doubled and tripled in his three trips vs. the A's right-hander. Norris' record dropped to 6-4 and the 25-year-old no longer led the league in ERA. Less than 900 miles north, New York's John was painting a master-piece. He would surrender harmless singles to Willie Horton and Tom Paciorek on the way to a 3-0 win over Seattle. John was sitting pretty at 8-2.By June 8, the Orioles had run off a modest 3-game winning streak, and maybe more importantly, jumped three spots in the division standings. Hoping for a sweep of Anaheim, Stone op-posed future Bird Don Aase. After making 91 starts from 1977-1980, Aase would never start another big league game in a career that would last another nine seasons. For the 1986 Orioles, Aase would earn a career-high 34 saves. This outing may told the Angels he was more suited to short relief. He didn't get out of the second inning.

Leadoff hitter Bumbry had three singles, a double and drove in five runs from the top of the order. Bumbry, would depart the contest in second place in the AL in on-base percentage (.438) and fourth in batting average (.351). Kiko Garcia, at the bottom of the lineup, pro-duced two singles, a double and four RBI.

All Stone had to do was throw a few curves and earn a quick win. Instead, his no-hitter vanished to the home team's leadoff hitter. Rick Miller played 15 seasons of Big League ball. A full dozen of those campaigns he was with the Red Sox trying to find playing time in an outfield of Carl Yastrzemski, Fred Lynn and Dwight Evans. Now with the Angels, Miller banged a two-bagger off of Stone. Two outs later, Jason Thompson tied the contest with another double. Carney Lansford's safety up the middle put the home team up a run at 2-1. Thompson and Lansford would figure in the scoring two frames later. Thompson's single to center chased Carew to third. Lansford's sac fly brought in Carew and knotted the contest at 3-3 in the third. Sammy Stewart would pick up his second win in the 13-8 slugfest despite walking a batter an inning in his six frames of work. The Angels staff would walk 11 Orioles in a game that closed in 3 hours, 39 minutes. The O's would have a six-run fifth inning and a four-run sixth. Stone was less than a month from his All-Star game start, but at this point he hardly looked like an All-Star. The good news was the Birds, after 52 games, had finally reached the .500 mark.

Friday night, June 12 marked the first matchup of the season between upstarts Stone and southpaw Rick Honeycutt. Honeycutt was four years into his career in which he made 287 starts. He wouldn't start a game after 1987, but by then he was in Oakland where Tony LaRussa was converting Honeycutt and former 20-game winner Dennis Eckersely into relievers. Eckersley would become one of the game's most feared closers, and Honeycutt found new life as a set-up man. The lefty from Tennessee would actually get into two games with the St. Louis Cardinals in 1997, 17 years after his tilt with Stone in 1980. He would pitch in nearly 800 Major League games during his 21-year run.

On June 12, Honeycutt had collected seven wins as he took on the O's and Stone. Both pitchers were on in the early innings. With two out in the fourth, O's designated hitter Benny Ayala connected with a home run with Singleton aboard. Stone had the lead for the first time at 2-1.

Batting only against left-handers, Ayala would bat a career-high 170 times and hit a solid .265 for the season. In his 28 at-bats in a Stone-started contest, his average jumped to .321.

"We would go out on the coast to Oakland, Angels and Seattle," Ayala recalled. "We would go 9-3. He consistently wanted the ball. We had four good starters in Martinez, Flanagan, McGregor and Palmer. He only had an opportunity as a fifth starter. He would pitch in the daytime, and he would throw his high fastball. He would make the umpire call the high strike."

The two pitchers settled in for awhile. In the sixth, Stone fanned Seattle's leading hitter, Bruce Bochte. Right fielder Joe Simpson also struck out. Third baseman Jim Anderson struck out a career-high 39 times in 1980 but that's only about once every 10 at-bats. He grounded the ball to DeCinces for a quick 1-2-3 frame. In the eighth, the O's stirred up some trouble. Bumbry cranked a one-out triple. But shortstop Garcia couldn't get him home on a bounce out. An ensuing rundown pinned down the Birds' best baserunner before he reached the plate. Garcia scooted to second and watched as Singleton strolled to the plate. One curve ball later and the Orioles led 4-1. It was Singleton's 10th homer of the season.

"I made a bad pitch to Singleton," Honeycutt told the *Seattle Times*. "A hanging curveball. I threw Ayala a high fastball away. But he is strong and reached out for it."

Stone began warming up for the ninth inning when he heard the crowd of more than 10,000 let out a cheer.

"When you are losing 4-1," Stone said. "I guess you cheer for volcanoes."

Stone finished victory No. 7 with a flourish. He caught leadoff hitter Julio Cruz looking at strike three.

"We didn't hit him," said Seattle manager Darrell Johnson. "He had good control and he threw sliders, curves, forkballs. He was tough."

In the visitor's dugout the winning manager was impressed as well.

"The complete game couldn't have come at a better time," Weaver told the *Sun*. "And we haven't seen enough of Dr. Long Ball. We've been seeing real doctors instead."

Weaver wasn't joking. Ayala was in the lineup in place of Gary Roenicke, who was saddled with a broken wrist.

Stone's fifth win in a row gave pushed the Birds back to the .500 mark (28-28).

The Cy Young race was affected on this day. At County Stadium, Royals lefty Larry Gura moved to 8-2 with a 4-3 matinee win over the Brewers. Cecil Cooper's two-run ninth-inning homer off of Dan Quisenberry left his team one run short.

Saturday night in the Kingdome was another date in which the pennant race got away from the Birds. In Oakland, Brian Kingman took a one-run lead to the top of the ninth. The A's right-hander had one out to go for a 1-0 victory over the Yanks. Bobby Murcer had other plans as he deposited his sixth homer of the campaign to make a victor out of Ed Figueroa. Fireballer Rich Gossage picked up his eighth save.

Meanwhile in Seattle, the O's McGregor was on the hill, and had four runs to work with heading to the third inning. Ayala's fifth- inning homer made it 6-3. The home half of the fifth decided this contest. Seattle's offense produced two homers, a triple and three singles on the way to six runs. The O's fell 9-8.

It must be noted that following this lost contest, the Baltimore Orioles posted the Majors' best mark (72-32) the rest of the season.

Trailing John, Gura and Norris in victories, seven-game winner Stone prepared to take the mound for a Tuesday night contest with the Angels. His opponent was 6-foot-6, 235-pound right-hander Dave Frost. Like the Orioles, Frost stood out in 1979. He won 16 games and finished with a solid ERA of 3.57. The first three hitters in the Angels' lineup reached base. Rick Miller took a pitch to the opposite field for a single. Both Fred Patek and Rod Carew walked. And so did pitching coach Ray Miller. He met Stone on the mound to try and talk him out of a bad performance.

"Ray told me to take my time a little bit," Stone said. "He said he thought I was rushing things. At that time, I knew I had good arm strength, and if I could survive the first, I was going to have a good ballgame."

Jason Thompson strode to the plate. The left-handed hitter was in his 25th game in an Angels uniform after arriving from Detroit in a deal for Al Cowens.

Stone's curve ball made Thompson the first strikeout victim of the game. Carney Lansford's fly ball chased home Miller with the game's first run but Joe Rudi popped to first baseman Eddie Murray to limit the rally to just the one run. The contest was tied at 2-2 in the sixth when Murray cracked his 10th homer. It also extended the switch-hitter's hitting streak to 14 games. Bumbry would follow in the seventh inning with a rare blast over the center field fence. A blast is a generous description; it barely cleared the wall and center fielder Bobby Clark's glove.

"The ball probably just jarred out of Clark's glove when his arm went over the fence," Bumbry told the *Sun*. "I have no complaints. I'll take it."

Stone (8-3) would pitch another complete game. He struck out 11 Angels in the 5-3 victory. Again, it was his overhand curve ball that messed up the timing of the Angels' hitters.

"I felt strong," Stone told the *Los Angeles Times*. "I was mad at myself for digging myself into some holes."

"A curveball pitcher has got to throw curves," Weaver told the Sun. "The funny thing is when he throws the fastball then, it goes by them when he wants it to. It might not be that fast but it looks like Bob Feller's when they are looking for the curve."

"Earl was very superstitious," Singleton said. "If you are doing well, he will stick with you. He was on such a roll. Steve was a good pitcher who was very intelligent. He knew what he wanted to do; he just couldn't get his body to do it."

Center fielder Clark led the strikeout parade at Memorial Stadium, fanning three times. Only Carew and Patek dodged the Stone fan machine. Six of those strikeout victims came in the Angels' final four at-bats.

"That was seven right-handed batters and a good curveball," Stone told the *Times*.

On the night of June 21, Stone took the mound, in search of his seventh straight victory. More than 28,000 were on hand to witness the new star battle a Mariners southpaw named Dave Roberts. This 35-year-old lefty had won 17 games for the 1973 Houston Astros. But in 1980, Roberts was in the twilight of his solid, if unspectacular career, and he would make only four starts all season. Still, he matched Stone pitch-for-pitch for three full innings.

In the home half of the fourth inning, first baseman Murray had seen enough. Hitting from the right-handed batter's box, Murray connected for a three-run homer, his 12th of the season. It was 3-0 in the fourth.

It was soon 6-0 in the fifth and 9-0 in the sixth. Jim Beattie would lose 15 games for Seattle in 1980, and was clearly no help in this contest. The right-hander retired one hitter and was charged with three earned runs. In the meantime, Baltimore's right-hander was breezing. In earning his ninth victory of the campaign, Stone surrendered a single and double to Danny Meyer. There were three more harmless singles. His third straight complete game featured just two walks and seven punch-outs. The Mariners would send a runner to third against the O's latest ace in just the opening frame and the ninth. The night before, Ted Cox had clocked a three-run homer in the ninth inning to stun loser Palmer and the Birds. In his trip to the plate in the sixth inning, Cox walloped two long foul balls before Stone nearly decked him with a fastball in the direction of his skull.

"The pitch that knocked him down just got away from me," Stone said. "I wasn't trying to knock him down. I never throw at hitters."

A Stone curve sent Cox back to the dugout.

"This is by far the best sequence of games I've had," Stone told the *Sun*. "I had good command of my breaking ball. I had better rhythm and I knew I was going to get the ball over. I felt I would throw strikes with all my pitches."

Stone discussed his winning streak with the *Washington Post*.

"Sure, it was 1967 when I was in Cleveland Class A," Stone said of his groove. "That was the last time. No, seriously, though, I've never been this good of groove in the Major Leagues."

The Mariners were no match for this hot pitcher.

"Seattle is no pushover now," Stone told the *Post*. "They've got (Juan) Beniquez, , Dan Meyer, (Tom) Paciorek in the middle of that lineup. They've got some punch. I'm just in a pretty good groove right now. And the Orioles are giving me four, five runs a ball game – nine tonight. It's hard to lose with that kind of support."

As usual, Weaver had plenty to say following this one. How could he explain the emergence of Stone, who was quickly becoming the staff ace?

"It's confidence," Weaver told the *Sun*. "When you've got it going you don't mind throwing the ball right to the center."

The top four hitters in the O's lineup (Bumbry, Dauer, Singleton and Murray) combined for eight hits, four runs and eight RBI in the rout.

Unlike the rest of his pitching staff, Stone had little trouble with the Seattle hitters in 1980.

"I seem to have good breaking stuff against them," Stone told the *Seattle Times*. "But I'll tell you, they're getting tougher. And nine runs takes a lot of pressure off of you. That three-run homer from Eddie Murray in the fourth was a big lift for everybody."

Seattle manager Darrell Johnson would lose his job before the season concluded. He was around long enough to appreciate Stone' work.

"We always struggle with Stone," Johnson told the *Seattle Times*.

Stone also took time to handicap what he surmised was a pennant race in the AL East.

"That one helped us win the sixth in seven tries," he said. "Everyone thinks the Yankees are in already. I don't. Remember the 1964 Phillies blew a 10-game lead with only a couple of weeks to go. The Yanks will hit a cold streak, and if we get hot at that time, we could catch them. We're ready to start streaking. We are a better ball club than we have shown. We'll get hot in the second half."

This was one hot pitcher who had peeked into the future with uncanny precision. Stone was an impressive 9-3 after this win. He was also named the American League Player of the Week for his two complete game victories during the seven-day period.

"He started concentrating on just his fastball and curveball," Scott McGregor said. "And he was lights out. It was incredible. He had a great curveball and a great fastball. He just mowed the league down. It was just his year. He really kind of simplified things. And that really helped him."

Saturday night in New York was the perfect time to see two Cy Young candidates go head-to-head. For New York, it was nine-game winner John. Matching him on this night was Oakland's eight-game winner Norris. First baseman Jim Spencer remained hot with the bat. He deposited a Norris pitch over the wall for a three-run dinger in the opening frame. However, neither pitcher was all that sharp. Like Flanagan five days earlier, John couldn't figure out the weak-hitting Mario Guerrero. The Oakland shortstop tripled to center and scored to pull Oakland within 4-3 in the fourth. Both pitchers settled in from there. The plate wasn't touched again until Nettles deposited his 11th round-tripper leading off the eighth inning. Only three Yanks managed hits off Norris on this night but it was enough to pin the fifth loss of the season on him. John surrendered three Rickey Henderson hits but earned win No. 10 in the 5-3 triumph. Gossage picked up save No. 10 in New York's ninth win in a row.

June 26, 1980

American League East	W	L	Pct.	GB
New York	44	24	.647	—
Milwaukee	38	29	.567	5½
Boston	37	31	.544	7
Detroit	35	30	.538	7½
Baltimore	36	32	.529	8
Cleveland	33	33	.500	10
Toronto	31	34	.477	11½

Pitching Matchup

Toronto (Jim Clancy 6-3, 2.32) at Baltimore (Steve Stone 9-3, 3.46)

10

Uncle Charlie

After McGregor and Palmer stopped a struggling Toronto club (31-35), the Blue Jays trotted out ace Jim Clancy in the series finale in Baltimore. At home in 1980, Stone would fashion a 14-4 mark. On this Thursday night, he set search for his eighth straight victory.

Clancy, who would win 128 games in his 13 years in a Jays uniform, entered this contest with the league's third-best ERA (2.59). That mark was slightly better than Oakland's Mike Norris but trailed both the Royal's Larry Gura and Chicago's Britt Burns.

His ERA took a bruising in the first inning. With barely 13,000 in attendance this night, Al Bumbry led off with a single. He advanced to second on a wild pitch. Kiko Garcia's single chased Bumbry home with the game's first run. Singleton flied out but Murray bounced one to right, sending Garcia to third. The rally continued as the left-handed specialists dialed in on Clancy. Terry Crowley and John Lowenstein completed the onslaught with run-scoring singles. Clancy departed seven hitters into the contest.

No doubt Stone smelled blood after that. The Blue Jays failed to threaten Stone for most of the game. The one exception was 20-year-old rookie Lloyd Moseby's homer to lead off the fifth inning. Moseby's blast was the first fence-clearing blast that Stone would give up in more than four games. The O's pitcher didn't blink after the home run pitch and fanned two of three in the both the sixth and eighth frames. The 4-1 victory gave the O's ace a 10-3 mark with his eighth straight victory.

"I had pretty good command of my pitches again," Stone said. "And scoring three runs in the first inning also made a big difference."

The pitch count in this victory was 133. Pitching coach Ray Miller counted 74 curveballs that night in Baltimore.

"That's a record," Miller told the *Sun*. "It beats the old one by one. It's a lot of curves. It's almost too many, but Steve is throwing it very well right now."

Stone's curveball was touched up for a double by Al Woods and two singles each by Damaso Garcia and Alfredo Griffin, but none of those players would touch home plate.

"It's a pretty good curveball," Stone said. "When I'm throwing it well, it has a good rotation. And a hitter can't stand up there and plant his feet because I vary the speed on it."

Stoddard recalled the trouble batters had with the Stone curve.

"The hitters knew the curveball was coming," Stoddard told this writer. "They still couldn't hit it, though. If he threw 100 pitches, 70 would be curveballs. He had a great curveball. That was his pitch. I don't think he really had a change-up. He changed speeds so much on the curve. He threw two- or three-speed curveballs for strikes. He took a different approach. He didn't make mistakes with his fastball."

The bullpen could see that ball breaking even from behind the fence.

"Steve always had a great curveball," Tippy Martinez said "If anything he probably threw a lot more strikes. It was a combination ofn being on a team that stresses defense as well as pitching. You can't take anything away from Steve. He had a good breaking ball and good command of the breaking ball. And if you can throw it behind in the count, you are going to be successful."

Pitching coach Miller also made a few adjustments in Stone's game plan. There was no more waiting around for this rock to throw the ball. Miller made it simple: Take the baseball in hand and fire it towards the the man in the mask in good order.

"He's had four complete games since he speeded up," Miller told the *Sun*. "When you are pitching quickly, it gets the defense ready to go."

This seemingly easy conquest of the Jays did have a bump along the way. Stone injured his left side fielding Griffin's first inning chopper. Trainer Ralph Salvon came to the rescue.

"Ralph straightened it out by about the fifth inning," Stone said.

Of course, putting runs on the board early made Stone's workload that much easier.

"We scored early in the game so he was the kind of guy who got the ball and knew what to do," Dauer said. "We were very good behind pitchers like that."

Stone's complete game effort featured nine punch-outs. Moseby may have launched his third homer of the season, but his other three at-bats versus Stone produced one force out and two strikeouts. Damaso Garcia also fell victim to the Stone breaking ball as the Blue Jays' second-baseman fanned twice. Only Barry Bonnell and Alfredo Griffin managed to avoid the strikeout pitch on June 26.

"Most of my strikeouts tonight were on curveball," Stone told the *Capitol Register*. "They were looking for it but they couldn't adjust to it."

Still, after Roy Howell opened the top of the ninth with his second hit of the contest, manager Weaver made a trip to the mound. This gesture did not meet with approval from the faithful on 33rd Street.

"The booing was pretty nice," Stone told the AP. "Last year at this time, they were booing my every appearance on the mound."

Weaver had no intention of pulling his streaking hurler. Stone was in line for his fourth consecutive complete game – something he hadn't repeated since he posted a 2.98 ERA for the 1972 Giants.

"If we had been ahead by only two runs, I probably would have considered taking him out," Weaver told the Associated Press. "I figured he might be close to running out of gas after four complete games. If I had taken him out, you really would have heard some boos."

Toronto manager Bobby Mattick would guide the Jays for 268 games in two seasons (the second season shortened by the 1981 strike). His team won less than 39 percent of the time. But the former National League infielder could judge a good breaking pitch.

"He has great rotation on his slow curve," Mattick told the AP. "Combine that with the fact he can throw the fastball by you and he has good control and it's not hard to see why he has 10 wins."

Stone, however, found himself scratching his head to figure out why he dominated the Blue Jays.

"You'd be surprised," Stone said. "Their line-up is not quite as easy as my record says. I got good pitches to (Alfredo) Griffin and (Lloyd) Moseby at key time and on (John) Mayberry once. A hit here and a hit there to those guys could have made the difference."

This victory completed a three-game sweep of the Jays. Baltimore was a season-high five games above the .500 mark (37-32). With only three AL games on tap this night, the Birds pulled to within 7.5 games of the idle Yanks. Still, fifth place was nothing to feel good about. A five-game road trip was next up with scheduled runs through Boston and Toronto.

Also on June 27, Mike Norris tossed a four-hitter at the visiting White Sox and moved to 9-5 on the season with the 3-1 victory. Norris had not beaten the White Sox dating back to 1977.

"I've had a lot of trouble with my curveball lately," Norris told the *Chicago Tribune.* "But I was getting it over tonight. I'm glad to see it's back because it will mean more strikeouts for me. There is no way anyone will be able to sit around and wait for my fastball."

Also on this night, the Dodgers torched San Francisco's Vida Blue on the way to an 8-0 win. Los Angeles southpaw Jerry Reuss pitched the season's only no-hitter.

When the night of June 30 closed, the American League had two 11-game winners: Tommy John and Steve Stone. At 37-years-old, John was coming off a season in which he won 21 games for a team that finished in fourth place, 13.5 games behind the AL champions from Baltimore. Tommy John was a marvel at 37.

The other 11-game was five years John's junior. Stone had pitched for the best team in the AL in 1979 yet won 10 fewer games. In Toronto, he would equal his entire previous season's total.

The 1980 season also marked the Major League debut of one Luis Leal of the Toronto Blue Jays. He would open his career with three wins in 80 games and close with three wins in 1985. In between, the Venezuelan would post 46 more victories in a Jays uniform. Leal watched his chances for a quick lead vanish into the glove of third sacker DeCinces. With former slugger John Mayberry stationed at first base following a free pass, Doug Ault laced a laser down the the third-base line. That's when DeCinces went into his Brooks Robinson act. His backhand of the shot and follow-up toss to Dauer at second began a quick 5-4-3 double play.

End of rally.

"That play might have turned the game around," Weaver said in the *Evening Sun*. . "If that ball gets through, who knows what might happen."

Leal retired one Orioles hitter in the third inning before departing. By that time, Dauer had two singles to his credit and Stone and club was up 3-0. By the fifth, Stone had allowed the Jays one Barry Bonnell single. When reliever Jesse Jefferson retired Bumbry to close the fifth, it was 7-0. With the hottest pitcher in the AL mowing down the home team, Stone's 11th win was a safe bet. After six innings at Exhibition Stadium, the 18,000 in attendance probably were nursing their O'Keefe beers and wondering why this sport had even bothered to cross the border. In the sixth, the one-hitter turned swiftly into a three-hitter.

Alfredo Griffin went the opposite way with a single that Lowenstein stopped in left. Griffin was in the midst of a career year. In 1980, he totaled 15 three-baggers, a number that would only tie him with Kansas City's Willie Wilson for the league lead. Damaso Garcia, batting from the right-hand side also poked a single to Lowenstein. The Jays had their first threat of the contest.

Up stepped left fielder Al Woods, who hit a tailor-made double play ball to second base. Dauer stood his ground at second and made two outs with it and that rally was extinguished rather quickly.

In the seventh, Stone showed some signs of tiring. After Stone fooled Ault on a third strike, the home team loaded the bases with two singles and a free pass. Again, Griffin came up and hit the ball the other way. This time, Lowenstein collared it before it hit the ground. With a seven-run lead, Stone was ready to take a seat and watch the rest of the contest.

"I started to run out of gas in the fifth inning," Stone told the *Evening Sun*. "And then I had two tough innings in a row. After four straight complete games, and another start coming up in three days (in Boston), it didn't seem to be the time to push it."

Manager Weaver didn't argue with his new ace.

"I'm the kind of guy who doesn't like to disturb things," Weaver told the *Evening Sun*. "But Steve said early he was wearing out. He's been piling up a lot of innings lately."

Bumbry tripled and Dauer doubled in a two-run eighth inning as Stone sat down and prepared to pocket his ninth straight victory. He would have been better served by checking out the nightlife outside the ballpark. Both Tippy Martinez and Tim Stoddard forgot the pitching book on Ault. In his last year in the Majors, Ault would hit an uninspiring .236, thus signaling it was time to find another profession. However, on this night, Ault would greet both relievers with two-run doubles in the three-run eighth and four-run ninth. He would actually collect 28 percent of his season total RBI (15) in those two frames. Tippy would be charged with six earned runs in 1⅔ innings. All four Toronto runs came after two outs in the ninth. Stone's win was finally secured when Stoddard fanned Garth Iorg to end the late rally. The bullpen had nearly blown Stone's winning streak away. But the 9-7 win made these poor performances that much easier to swallow.

Stone's run of complete games had kept the O's bullpen well rested. It also kept them twiddling their thumbs out in right field. Martinez tried to explain that to the *Evening Sun*.

"It's part of a reliever's job," Martinez said. "Sometimes, you are going to run into a situation like that. But there is only one thing to look at it. We won the game and I got a chance to see new hitters. I really needed that. It's been so long. Sure, I gave up six hits and six runs but the important thing is I got some work."

Stone sat nervously until the final out was secured.

"I didn't think about the tying run being at the plate in the ninth, Stone told the *Toronto Star*. "I just thought about Tim Stoddard getting the last guy out. He did."

With his 11th win in the bag, the Toronto press wanted to talk with the All-Star manager, Baltimore's iconic Earl Weaver.

July 4, 1980

American League East	W	L	Pct.	GB
New York	49	26	.653	—
Milwaukee	42	32	.568	6½
Detroit	40	32	.556	7½
Baltimore	41	34	.547	8
Boston	39	35	.527	9½
Cleveland	36	37	.493	12
Toronto	32	41	.438	16

Pitching Matchup

Boston (Mike Torrez 4-8, 4.71) at Baltimore (Steve Stone 12-3, 3.10)

11

Campaigning

"I can't say anything about the All-Star pitchers because it's illegal," Weaver said. "It's still before the whatchamacallit release date, but I'd say that with 11 wins, it gives him a pretty good shot at making the team. If someone else was managing the All-Star team, I'd be saying Stone should be on it."

Stone wasn't concerned about any illegalities.

"I'd be surprised if I wasn't selected," Stone said.

The right-hander closed the best June of his Major League career with a spotless 5-0 record and a dazzling 2.47 ERA. He was selected as the American League's Pitcher of the Month. In August 1975, Palmer won six of seven decisions to also earn this award.

As the calendar made its turn to July, the American League East standings were becoming clearer. The first-place Yankees had the best record in the Majors (47-25). The improving O's were six games up on the .500 mark (39-33) but still mired in fourth place and trailing by eight full games. On Canada Day in Toronto, the Orioles caravan was again riding on four wheels. Stone had 11 of the team's 39 wins. Oakland's Norris and Detroit's Jack Morris joined the 10-win club the next night (July 2). To no one's surprise, Norris went all 10 innings in County Stadium for his victory. Gorman Thomas and Don Money each fanned twice against the A's ace in the 5-3 win.

The Red Sox had come off a 16-10 June and pushed to within one game of fourth-place Baltimore in the loss column as Independence Day arrived. The Sox's first task was to find a way to topple the streaky Stone. The winning streak was nine games as Stone walked leadoff hitter Rick Burleson. No problem. Jerry Remy lined hard to Belanger, and Burleson was doubled off first.

Bumbry walked to open the O's half of the first facing Red Sox seven game loser Mike Torrez. Dauer, Murray, Singleton and Crowley reached Torrez for hits in the three-run inning and out went Torrez and in his place came Dick Drago.

For the campaign, Torrez would finish 0-3 vs. his ex-teammates with a dreadful 13.50 ERA. He would also take a seven-game losing streak vs. Baltimore into the 1981 season.

In typical Stone fashion, the bats were firecracker-hot and he could settle in and throw his curveball. It was 6-0 by the third inning. Entering the fifth, Stone had allowed just one Carl Yastrzemski hit. The fifth was a different story. Dave Stapleton's lone hit in the game was a run-scoring triple in this frame. Center fielder Garry Hancock drove home Stapleton when he pulled a single to right. The visitors had a pair of quick runs.

"My curveball wasn't as good tonight as it has been in some earlier games," Stone told the *Boston Globe*. "I threw 116 pitches on a very hot night."

In his modesty, Stone neglected to point out that Hancock was the lone Red Sox hitter to reach him for more than one hit. The Sox did creep a run closer in the sixth. Tony Perez, 10 full seasons removed from his clash with the Orioles in the 1970 World Series, entered the contest in first place in the AL in RBI (60). At the end of the campaign, the 38-year-old first baseman would only lead the league in double play grounders (25). However, in the sixth, he launched his 11th homer of the season.

"He gave me a curve," Perez told the *Globe*. "And I was ready. He has a good curveball and it makes his fastball tougher. That is why so many guys pop him up, because they are looking curve and can't handle the fastball."

Perez didn't sweat much this season when the Orioles pitchers came after him. He hit a cool .478 with six homers and 17 RBI. Two of those long balls were surrendered by Stone.

The Sox reached Stone for three singles in the seventh but managed no runs. This mini-barrage was enough to tell Weaver his star was done for the night. In came Stoddard with seven outs to go.

"Earl (Weaver) didn't want to let it get away," Stone said in the *Globe*. "And I'm glad he brought in Tim (Stoddard). He made a big pitch on (Carlton) Fisk and saved the game."

With the bases juiced, the Sox catcher popped a Stoddard pitch straight up and into Belanger's glove for the final out in the seventh.

Weaver sensed the heat was getting to Stone.

"He's pitched a lot of innings in the last month," Weaver told the *Globe*. "I took him out of a 9-0 game in Toronto on Monday for the same reason."

Stone's 10th consecutive victory was by a 10-3 margin. Dauer and Crowley led the offense with three hits each.

"I was missing with the curve a little," Stone told the *Sun*. "And I wasn't throwing as many strikes with it as other nights. I didn't have the greatest stuff in the world this time and Earl didn't want to let it get away. It was just like the beginning of the season for me."

Now 12-3 on the campaign, the journeyman was well on his way to making his first All-Star Game appearance. And with his manager in charge of the pitching rotation, his chances of starting the contest for the AL looked bright.

"At this point, it's definitely the thing to do," Weaver told the *Sun*. "Steve's pitching good and no one in the league will have more than 12 wins. Everything points to doing it. And I can't see any reason not to do it."

In typical Weaver double-speak, the O's boss had made comments that seemed impossible a year ago. His fifth starter had the most wins in the American League. After his World Series appearance in 1979 and this amazing run of victories, the erudite Stone did, in fact, get it.

"The team has played very well behind me all year," Stone told the *Post*. "They haven't made any mistakes. The defense has been great and I've had some runs to work with. It just seems everything has fallen in place for me."

Stone recalled a meeting with the solemn Scott McGregor.

"McGregor got a no-decision in a game where he was ahead," Stone told the *Post*. "The bullpen let in a couple of runs. We came back to win. I said, 'It's pretty tough to let it slip away.'

"He said, 'It was OK.' What amazed me, he was serious. A lot of people I have been around would have been angry. His attitude has really helped me."

Years later, McGregor noted being on winner made all the difference in the world to Stone.

"When he came over, the whole year, he was kind of dumbfounded by the way he did things," McGregor said. "He had not been on teams that had been in a race. He was amazed that we really did pitch for the team to win."

Even a double-digit winning streak couldn't knock his feet off the ground.

"I've always been a person to whom the game was not a life-or-death situation," Stone told the *Times*. "Even when it was the sole means of my support. I always felt if I lost, I lost, and I'd get them the next time. When I was 8-8, I was happy, and I'm happy now. I'm really enjoying this season. I've had people come up to me and say the winning streak must really be a lot of pressure. But it really isn't for the simple reason I wasn't supposed to have it."

1980 All-Star Game

National League Lineup

Name (Club)	Pos.	AVG	HR	RBI	SB	OBP	SLG
Davey Lopes (LA)	2b	.236	5	21	13	.322	.323
Reggie Smith (LA)	cf	.328	15	51	4	.397	.553
Dave Parker (PIT)	rf	.286	10	43	8	.325	.443
Steve Garvey (LA)	1b	.291	18	66	4	.324	.488
Johnny Bench (CIN)	c	.280	11	33	2	.356	.492
Dave Kingman (CHI)	lf	.264	10	33	2	.315	.479
Ken Reitz (STL)	3b	.282	4	33	0	.311	.381
Bill Russell (LA)	ss	.291	3	20	8	.319	.394
J.R. Richard (HOU)*	p	.132	1	3	0	.132	.237
Bob Welch (LA)	p	.194	0	0	0	.216	.222

*Richard was pulled after two innings and did not bat.

Pitching Matchup

American (Steve Stone, Baltimore, 12-3, 3.10) at National (J.R. Richard, Houston, 10-4, 1.96)

12

All-Star Break

On July 31, 1961, future U.S. Senator Jim Bunning hurled three scoreless, hitless innings of the second All Star game of the season. The Tigers ace registered line-outs off the bats of Maury Wills and Orlando Cepeda but still managed to retire nine straight National League hitters.

Five years later, another Tigers hurler took the mound for the AL. Two years away from making history with his 31-win season, Detroit right-hander Dennis McLain fanned three, including Willie Mays and Henry Aaron, on the way to a perfect three frames of work in the 1966 All-Star Game. McLain and the AL would drop a 2-1 extra-inning decision to the NL despite the magical glove work and three hits of game MVP Brooks Robinson.

On July 8,1980, the 5-foot-10 Stone made his first appearance in a Major League All-Star Game at Los Angeles' Dodger Stadium. His mound opponent was the 6-foot-8 J.R. Richard. The Astros flame-thrower was 10-4 with a league-leading 1.96 ERA. Obviously no one

would guess that the 30-year-old right-hander would never win another Major League game. A devastating stroke would silence his career 22 days later.

"I thought one day I might get a chance to play in an All- Star
Game," Stone told the *Sun*.

"It's a tremendous thrill making it, but starting is something I
couldn't hope for in my wildest dreams. I thought maybe Steve Carlton would start for the National League and then everyone could
have said Steve Carlton against Steve Who?"

Stone would face a National League lineup that featured four hitters playing on their home field. Second baseman Davey Lopes and
right-fielder Reggie Smith batted one-two. The switch-hitter Smith
was second in his league in on-base percentage (.397) and third in
slugging percentage (.553). Cleanup hitter Steve Garvey was in the
midst of three consecutive 200 plus hits seasons. The LA first-
baseman entered the classic tops in baseball in RBI (66). He also was
third in at-bats (330) and hits (96). Shortstop Billy Russell completed the Dodgers' foursome.

Dave Parker would hit third for Chuck Tanner's NL club. And in
two plate appearances in the 1979 series against Stone, the Cobra had
singled and doubled. Popular Reds catcher Johnny Bench was in the
fifth slot for the senior league. Chicago's tall slugger Dave Kingman,
would hit sixth.

"I've faced every hitter in the NL lineup," the former Cubs and
Giants hurler said "But there's no advantage. If I throw strikes, I'll
get the batters out. Bad pitches and they'll hit me. The most difficult
batter I had to face in the National League was Ted Simmons and
he's not playing."

Was Stone referring to his June 22, 1975 loss in Busch Stadium?
The switch-hitting Simmons had drilled his ninth homer of the season off the Cubs right-hander in a 7-2 Cardinals victory. Or was the
date September 22, 1974? Stone was opposed by future Hall-of-
Famer Bob Gibson. Amazingly, the Cubs batted around against Gib-

son in the sixth inning. Gibson didn't get a decision in this contest at Busch Stadium.

Neither did Stone. Simmons greeted Stone with a two-run dinger in the opening frame. It was the switch-hitter's 19th homer of the campaign. Simmons would knock in four runs during a 6-5 Cardinal victory.

In all fairness, Simmons' lifetime slugging percentage against Stone was a cool .900.

During that 1974 campaign, Simmons hit three of his lifetime four homers versus Stone. That ranks him second all-time in long balls versus the O's overnight success.

The fans had spoken in their 10th election of All-Star players since the voting had been restored to the paying customers a decade earlier. If the players had held this privilege Stone would have faced a considerably different and more challenging offense. Leadoff hitter Lopes earned the most votes (3,862,403) of the participants. Still, his batting average had slumped below .240 entering the All-Star game. In a poll of players, the names of second basemen Manny Trillo (.318) and Phil Garner (.277) came up before Lopes.

At first base, Garvey was hitting a robust .293 with 18 homers and 65 RBI. That wasn't good enough for his fellow players. They pointed to St. Louis for 26-year-old first baseman Keith Hernandez. He was sixth in the NL in hitting (.320) but couldn't match Garvey in the power department. Russell was hitting .291 at the break and was voted to start at shortstop. But sitting in third place in the league was another Cardinal, Garry Templeton. He was the lone National Leaguer with more than 100 hits (111) and was batting .327. At third, the fans gave St. Louis a victory in the ballot box. But Ken Reitz was mired in a 2-for-33 slump that kicked off in late June. Reitz was still hitting a respectable .287. Ray Knight of Cincinnati was also selected to the team by manager Tanner and was batting .295.

Right-fielder Parker was on target for a strong season batting .288 with nine homers and 42 RBI. The fans, who spotted his solid gold throwing arm in the 1979 World Series, no doubt wished to see him battle Stone and the relievers in this contest. Players opted for another Cardinal (George Hendrick). And no wonder, his 17 homers and .310 average stood out. Left-fielder Kingman was still hitting .285 with 11 homers at the break. But the 6-foot-6 free-swinger was coming off that 0-for-9 performance versus Pittsburgh on July 6 when his Cubs lost 5-4 in 20 innings. To make matters worse, Kingman was still bothered by a shoulder injury suffered in late May. His season closed after 81 games. The players chose the Dodgers' Dusty Baker and his 18 homers. Finally, catcher Bench was hitting .266. Stone's nemesis, and the player's choice, the Cardinals' Simmons, was batting nearly 30 points higher.

Stone, who had never made an All-Star squad before, was given the starting assignment by his manager, Earl Weaver.

"I thought I might have a chance with the South Side Hitmen but I finished 12-8," Stone told this writer. "It really worked out in 1980. I had a 12-3 record. It helped that Earl was the manager and I was on perfect rest."

The National League had won eight straight All-Star classics. The last American League victory was dated July 13, 1971. And the AL had to erase a 3-0 deficit in to earn that 6-4 victory.

"Everybody in this clubhouse wanted to win this game," Stone said. "They are tired of hearing all that stuff about the American League losing eight straight All-Star games."

The first-place Yankees had some opinions on why the AL was on a losing streak. Tommy John had been an All-Star in 1978 representing the Los Angeles Dodgers.

"When I was with the National League, it was like they were there for blood," John told the *New York Times*. "It was a big thing for them. They came there, and they expected to win. It was the big guys, – the Stargells and Parkers and Benches who set the tone and said, 'We're going to win.'"

Bob Watson was a NL All-Star while playing for the Houston Astros in 1975.

"Those guys were up for the game," Watson said. "They wanted to win. It wasn't just another ballgame. They were really psyched. From the first pitch the guys were yelling, 'Let's show them who's best.'"

Luis Tiant was a three-time AL All-Star. And El Tiante had plenty of thoughts on the matter.

"I think the National League picks guys who can play complete," Tiant said. "They can hit, run, throw, hit the long ball, hit for RBI. The American League, they pick players you never heard of. Guys having good years, don't go. Guys hitting .150 go because the fans pick them. They just have so many guys over there who can do so many things."

Even American League President, Lee MacPhail, weighed in on the embarrassing subject. After all, losing 16 of 17 in All-Star play was certainly not something to proud of.

"Since I became president of the American League in 1974, I've been trying to give an explanation every year," MacPhail told the *New York Times*. "I started with scientific theories but that didn't work. Then I turned humorous. Then I began to make brave predictions. And I still don't know why."

Naturally, Stone had thoughts on the issue of why the AL just couldn't win the All-Star Game.

"Anything can happen in a game," Stone told the *New York Times*. "But I would admit that the National League has sent better players to the game the last few years, whatever the reason. But just look at all the young players in our league who aren't even 25-years-old.

"Guys like Alan Trammell and Willie Wilson, and you'll be seeing a change in the series in the next few years."

The AL's starting pitcher could look behind him and get a feel what it was like to have a lead in the AL East. Stone's infield defense was dominated by Yankees. There was Nettles at third, Bucky Dent at short and Willie Randolph at second. Reggie Jackson was in right.

The O's hottest pitcher was the lone starter from a team that nearly won the World Series the season before.

"I've played the game 12 years and never received any honors," Stone told the *Post*. "Now in the last two weeks, I've been selected the American League Player of the Week, the American League Pitcher of the Month and now the starting pitcher in the All-Star Game. I haven't sold my soul to the devil but I've had a hard time convincing my parents."

Unlike his Orioles has been accustomed to doing, the AL All-Stars didn't break out on top to give Stone an early lead as the 51st All-Star game opened play in Dodger Stadium. After Randolph opened the game grounding out to his NL counterpart, Lopes, Rod Carew coaxed a walk from Richard. The 34-year-old Carew, who would steal 23 bases for the Angels of 1980, tested the throwing arm of 32-year-old Johnny Bench. Both players would be in baseball's Hall-of-Fame by the early 1990s. Carew won this battle and stood at second base with one out in the first. He moved to third base on a grounder to second by Boston's Fred Lynn. This brought up Yankees' slugger Reggie Jackson. In his 21-year Hall-of-Fame career, Jackson hit .300 just once, in 1980, when he hit the .300 mark right on the nose. He also fanned 122 times. Richard blew down Jackson and sent Stone to the mound with no runs to work with.

Baseball players read papers, too. And, no doubt, some of the veterans in the National League might have been surprised to see the old Cub Stone on the mound. The word had certainly trickled down that the veteran had a curveball worth watching out for. But irony intervened and the curveball would take a back seat during Stone's once-in-a-lifetime chance. Here was a journeyman who had never come close to earning a spot on the All-Star team. And here he was starting the contest on national television. His adrenal gland was working overtime.

"When I first got out there, I really didn't have a really good curve," Stone said. "So, I went with my fastball and stayed with it. I was pumped up and stronger than usual. Stronger than I wanted to be."

Lopes was entering the twilight of his career after spending much of the 1970s as one of the premier second basemen in the National League. The 35-year-old second sacker would never again bat 500 or more times in a Major League season after the 1980 season. He had not batted against Stone since August 13, 1976 when his Dodgers invaded Wrigley for a Friday afternoon game, the first half of a doubleheader. It went 15 innings and Lopes went home 0-for-7. Stone went nine innings and then retired two hitters in the 10th inning before departing with no decision. Lopes was the last Dodger hitter he faced, retiring him a routine grounder. Less than four years later at Dodger Stadium, Lopes darted a Stone offering on the ground down the third base line and seemingly by the gifted Nettles at third. The Yankees' third baseman positively stole a sure extra-base hit from the startled Lopes.

There was one out.

The 56,000-plus fans sat down to watch the next Dodgers hitter stroll to the dish. Reggie Smith had spent the first seven years of his big league career in the suit of the Boston Red Sox. It was when he was with Boston that Smith homered off of Stone, in 1973. Smith was a career .333 hitter against Stone. This time, Smith connected with a Stone curveball and chased the man who replaced Smith in centerfield for the Red Sox back towards the wall. Fred Lynn collared the sphere, and two Dodgers were out. After two hitters, Stone knew his top pitch had taken the night off.

"Lopes hit a curve ball and Nettles made a great play at third," Stone told this writer. "And then Smith hit one to the wall. I then started throwing mostly fastballs. I threw 17 fastballs and seven curves and surprised some of the guys"

On Independence Day 1975, 25-year-old Dave Parker of the Pittsburgh Pirates drove in a first-inning run against Cubs right-hander Steve Stone. The Pirates would get two hits over the next eight innings. Stone won his sixth game of the season with a complete-game five-hitter. Parker's two hits vs. the Orioles' Stone in last year's World Series was more fresh on the minds of these two combatants when Parker loaded his 6-foot-5, 230-pound frame into the left-handed batter's box. Stone's rejuvenated fastball was waiting, and Parker was a strikeout victim for the inning's final out.

Three up and three down.

Second sacker Dauer recalled watching the All-Star game.

"All I remember is that he started the All-Star Game and struck out three guys on fastballs," Dauer said. "And he never threw a fastball in the 25 games he won. A lot of curveballs."

The designated hitter rule was no doubt made for Stone. In 219 trips to the plate in his National League days, Stone hit almost exactly .100. He had 20 singles and two doubles. In 96 of those plate appearances, Stone walked back to the dugout with his lumber in hand, striking out out 42 percent of the time. Less than four years removed from batting duties, manager Weaver stuck with Stone even though the AL had runners on the corners with two down in a tie game in the second. Richard cast an eye on the batter's box and blew Stone down for the third out of the second.

On Aug. 18, 1975, 26-year-old Dodgers first baseman Steve Garvey was in Wrigley Field for a daytime battle with Cubs right-hander Stone. Garvey popped one up behind the plate where Cubs receiver Steve Swisher secured for the first out of the second inning. Stone would hurl nine strong innings in a 3-1 loss to the Dodgers. Garvey wouldn't get the ball out of the infield. History was repeated somewhat when Garvey opened up the second frame for the National League. He popped one out. This time, it was catcher Carlton Fisk throwing off the mask in search of the foul ball. Garvey was out number one of the second.

"Steve Garvey never got any hits off me for some reason anyway," Stone told this writer.

Four up, four down.

"What typified his season was that All-Star Game," Roenicke said. "He just went in and blew away the hitters."

On Aug. 26, 1975, Cincinnati Reds catcher John Bench cracked his 25th homer of the season versus Stone in the sixth inning of another day game at Wrigley. The right-hander would again fail in a bid to secure his 12th win of the season as Joe Morgan singled home two runs in the visitor's ninth.

Five years removed from that battle in the midst of the Reds' heyday, Bench pushed one towards Dent at short. The Yankees infielder found the glove of first baseman Rod Carew for out number two.

"Bench took a fastball and grounded to short," Stone said. "He went back to the dugout and said, 'You threw me a fastball.'"

"I said, 'I threw you a fastball and you grounded to shortstop.'"

Five up, five down.

The two-strike fastball to Kingman had to be 10 feet tall. The free-swinger brought out his butterfly net and swung right through it for the final out of the second inning. Contrary to public opinion, the slugger Kingman did not strike out every time in his Major League career that spanned 16 seasons. Officially, it was 27 percent of the time.

Stone and Kingman were teammates on the successful Giants teams of the early 1970's. Kingman brought out the heavy lumber in 1972 when he blasted 29 homers. He also was second in the National League in whiffs (140). On April 29, 1972, Orioles-to-be Torrez (then with Montreal) and Stone (San Francisco) battled at Candlestick. Torrez won his first decision of the year on a complete game five-hitter. Stone went eight innings and allowed just five hits and one earned run. Kingman struck out three times and made an error.

"I struck out the last guy of each inning," Stone said. "That was Parker, Kingman and Bob Welch. Kingman struck out on the pitch over his head."

At 23-years-old, Dodgers right-hander Bob Welch was 10 years removed from his Steve Stone-like 1990 season. Of course, he would compile seven seasons of 13 or more wins before he had his remarkable 27-win season of 1990. And unlike Stone, he finished in the top 10 in the Cy Young Award sweepstakes twice prior to his breakout season.

Welch took the mound on his home field in the third inning. It was a rocky frame for sure. Willie Randolph singled and was promptly picked off at first by Welch. That move proved costly for the American League as Carew ripped a two-bagger the opposite way. With the play in front of him, Randolph would have had the option to test left-fielder Kingman's arm. Instead, Carew trotted into second base with a bases-empty double. After Fred Lynn struck out, Welch walked Reggie Jackson, uncorking a wild pitch on ball four. This put runners on the corners with two down for the slugger Ogilvie. He fanned.

Stone had one more inning to go in his first and final All-Star appearance, as the rules allow for a pitcher to go for a maximum of three innings. Stone was fortunate to miss perhaps the biggest National League star in Los Angeles. Philadelphia's Mike Schmidt was the NL MVP in 1980, hitting 48 homers for the eventual World Series champion Phillies. He was naturally voted to start at third for the National League, but a hamstring injury kept him out of action. In his place came a steady Cardinals third baseman named Ken Reitz. Like Stone, this was Reitz's first and only All-Star appearance. Reitz could match the slugger Schmidt in the batting department with his .287 mark. But the Phillies star was miles ahead in homers, leading 21-4. But would have Stone pitched around the Philadelphia monument?

Flash back to August 4, 1975 in Veterans Stadium. Cubs right-hander Stone faced Schmidt three times. He hit him once and fanned him twice. That all said, Schmidt still hit .278 against Stone, and touched him for two longballs in the 22 at-bats the two faced each other.

Reitz, on the other hand, wasn't peaking towards the All-Star game. His bat had grown silent since late June as he was bitten by a 2-for-33 slump. Stone's fastball tied Rietz up. A checked swing ground ball was the result, and Randolph threw him out easily.

Seven up, seven down.

Shortstop Russell was up next. The 31-year-old infielder would play every one of his 2,181 games in a Dodgers uniform. The eighth hitter in the National League lineup was still a threat. Of Russell's 23 doubles in 1980, 16 came prior to the All-Star game. He put the bat on the ball and skied to Ogilvie in left field for out No. 2.

Eight up, eight down.

All that stood between Stone and a perfect three innings of work was the pitcher Welch. Of course, this was the season in which the 23-year-old Dodgers pitcher hit a robust .243 in 70 at-bats, striking out just 13 times all year long. Stone made quick work of him on this night, however. It was Stone's third strikeout, and it completed his faultless pitching performance in the spotlight of the All-Star Game.

"He deserved the All-Star Game," Bumbry said. "It was one of those unusual years."

The rest of the 1980 All-Star Game went as expected. The AL lost. That was despite taking a 2-0 lead in the fifth when Fred Lynn deposited a Welch pitch over the right field wall with Carew on first. The American League's hitters struck out 11 times and fell for the ninth straight time, 4-2. The losing streak didn't dissolve until the 1983 season when Lynn's grand slam decided things early.

Stone's perfect outing naturally brought more attention to the surprising star.

"I was always tough in all-star games," Stone said in a *New York Times* feature. "In 1965, I pitched in an Ohio high school all-star game and did just that (have a perfect outing)."

Stone knew the NL sluggers were waiting for his breaking ball to come their way.

"Being primarily a breaking-ball pitcher, the National League guys were looking for the curveball," he told the *New York Times*. "So I threw a lot of fastballs. I'll sit back, and perhaps tomorrow or the next day, it will hit me as to what I have done."

Orioles pitching coach, Ray Miller, was mesmerized by his star pupil's performance in the All-Star Game.

"I was sitting at home watching him pitch in the All-Star Game," Miller told the *Milwaukee Journal*. "And I was getting so excited. When he was facing his third batterin the third inning, I got up on my chair and started screaming and jumping. My wife asked me why I was getting so excited, and I just said, 'How many times does a guy pitch three perfect innings in an All-Star Game?'"

Stone could have gone down in the books as the last pitcher to perform this task as All-Star managers have grown reluctant to have a pitcher throw the maximum three innings in this event. But six seasons later at the Houston Astrodome, a 15-game winner named Roger Clemens rolled through the National League lineup — nine up and nine down. Clemens, who was in the middle of his first of seven Cy Young Award seasons in 1986, may be the last to sit down nine in a row. Few others have been able to pitch three innings in an All-Star Game, much less come close to perfection.

In Clemens' three-inning gem in 1986, Mets fireballer Dwight Gooden and the Dodgers' Fernando Valenzeula each pitched three innings for the National League. Milwaukee's version of Valenzuela, portly left-handed Teddy Higuera went three innings in relief of Clemens. Gooden was touched for a Lou Whitaker homer. The 21-game winner from Los Angeles was clearly more effective. Valenzuela was 11-6 at the All-Star break and proceeded to tie an All-Star record with five strikeouts in a row. Cal Ripken was one of those victims. A Wade Boggs safety prevented a perfect outing by Valenzuela.

Brett Saberhagen was impressive in the 1987 All-Star game. The Royals right-hander also went the full three innings allowed. He surrendered just one hit, a two-bagger off the bat of eventual National League MVP Andre Dawson, who was making his first plate appearance since being beaned in the face by San Diego's Eric Show a week earlier. Later in the game, which went 13 innings, Cubs' closer Lee Smith came in to pitch. Smith walked none and struck out four in his three innings. His strikeout victims included Minnesota's Kirby Puckett (twice), Oakland's Mark McGwire and Toronto's Tony Fernandez. But Smith allowed singles to Texas' Larry Parrish and Boston's Dwight Evans.

In 1988 at Riverfront Stadium, Gooden finished his three innings of work for the NL. Gooden allowed three hits, including a Terry Steinbach solo homer.

In the 1994 All-Star Game at Pittsburgh's Three Rivers Stadium, Braves right-hander Greg Maddux went three innings vs. the American League. He was soon in trouble allowing back to back hits to Wade Boggs and Ken Griffey Jr. before White Sox star Frank Thomas singled home a run. Maddux promptly induced Joe Carter to hit a line drive right back at Maddux, who doubled up Thomas at first. Maddux then retired the last six men he faced.

The last pitcher to go three innings in an All-Star Game was Colorado's Aaron Cook, who lasted a scoreless but shaky three innings in a 15-inning affair at Yankee Stadium in 2008. Cook walked four batters (two of them intentionally) and allowed three hits, but somehow escaped with a scoreless outing.

Nine games out and fourth place was no place for the defending American League champs. At the All-Star break of 1979, the Birds were flying 18 games over the .500 mark. Some of the blame went to the O's batters. Bumbry was certainly pulling his weight (.321). He was in the top 15 in the league in hitting. Next up was Singleton's .285 mark. That barely slipped below 50th in the batting race. To be fair, teammate, Murray also sported that .285 mark and matched the O's right fielder with homers (12). With 32 more at-bats to work with, the first-sacker had knocked home seven more runs than Singleton (49). Dauer wasn't to be out-done. He was the third O's hitter with a .285 mark. However, he was still waiting for his initial round-tripper of the campaign.

July 12, 1980

American League East	W	L	Pct.	GB
New York	52	28	.650	—
Milwaukee	42	32	.563	7
Detroit	42	35	.545	8½
Baltimore	43	37	.538	9
Boston	42	38	.525	10
Cleveland	38	40	.487	13
Toronto	34	44	.436	17

Pitching Matchup

Kansas City (Renie Martin 8-5, 4.24) at Baltimore (Steve Stone 13-3, 3.00)

13

A classy guy

If the summer of 1980 was the time to catch Steve Stone's magical campaign on the mound, it also marked a season to catch a magician with a wood bat in Kansas City.

George Brett, the 27-year-old Royals third baseman, had come off a 1979 season of 42 doubles, 20 triples and 23 homers. A year later, Brett had been bitten by hand and wrist sprains and spent five weeks on the disabled list healing. When he was in the Royals lineup, Brett managed nothing but line drives. He was a legitimate threat to chase Ted Williams' unthinkable .406 mark from 1941.

The Royals had the league's best hitter and a robust 9.5 game lead in the AL West. They would boast of six hurlers who would win 10 or more games. The 10-game winner on the staff was a 6-4 right-hander named Renie Martin. The Royals invaded Memorial Stadium on Saturday night setting their sights on ending Stone's 10-game winning streak. After his perfect 9-for-9 outing in the All-Star Game, Stone battled this tough customer.

Leadoff hitter Willie Wilson beat one on the ground to shortstop Garcia. Hal McRae did the same thing except he pushed a bouncer that troubled DeCinces at third. Scorecards read "E-5," and there was one on and one out for the best hitter in baseball. But this was Steve Stone's magical year, too. Another ground ball sprayed out, this time in the direction of the sure-handed Dauer at second. The inning was over following the twin killing.

"You've got to give Stone credit," Royals manager Jim Frey said in the *Kansas City Star*. "He is at his best in this stadium. And he has been one of the finest pitchers in the American League since the All-Star break of last season."

The right-hander Martin didn't flinch at first. He retired four straight O's hitters before John Lowenstein strolled to the plate in the second inning. The 33-year-old had provided a spark when he arrived from Texas in 1978. Not known for his power stroke, the left-handed batter would connect for 24 homers during the 1982 campaign. But as of July 12, 1980, Lowenstein's homer collection for the season was empty. One swing later, he had his first dinger and Stone had his first lead of the game.

"Walls and balls."

That's how Lowenstein summed up his career to the *Sun*. "Left-field walls that I crashed into and balls that wouldn't go out."

Stone had surrendered a single and a walk in the second but averted trouble by fanning Darrell Porter, Frank White and Amos Otis. The three-strike call on Otis was a rare one according to Stone.

"Otis has hit me as well as anybody," Stone told the *Star*. "In fact, it's ridiculous the way he hits me."

The date was July 31, 1973. Stone would lose a complete-game seven-hitter and fan eight Royals. He would also lose his ninth game of the year versus four wins. In the 2-1 loss at Comiskey, 26-year-old Amos Otis would double and triple.

Stone, and for that matter, Martin, breezed through the early innings. Porter fanned again to open the fourth and Stone had notched his sixth K. In the fifth, White bounced into a double play and Stone felt a pain in his back.

"Things were really rolling the first four innings," Stone said, according to the next morning's *Sun*. "But on a pitch to White, I hurt my back a little. During the season, Ralph (trainer Ralph Salvon) has been able to pop it back in the clubhouse between innings. But not tonight. It was a little extra tight."

The result of this back wrenching was immediate. With two down in the fifth, Brett, Porter and Willie Aikens each received free passes. The sacks were loaded for the aforementioned Otis. With the sacks jammed, Otis popped a ball up to left field, whichLowenstein squeezed.

"This time, I lucked out," Stone said in the *Sun*.

Murray cracked a two-run double in the sixth to give ailing Stone some relief. Willie Wilson would lead the AL in three-baggers 1980. One of his 15 triples came in the Royals' seventh inning and it ended Stone's bid for a shutout. Wilson died on third when McRae bounced out.

It was Tippy time. Martinez was summoned in the eighth and asked to retire the left-handed batters in manager Jim Frey's lineup.

"Things kind of came into place for Steve," Martinez said. "Everything went right. Steve always had a great curveball. If anything, he probably threw a lot more strikes. It was a combination on being on a team that stresses defense as well as pitching. Steve didn't have a great fastball. He probably had an average fastball for guys in the Major Leagues. So he had to have something that he could throw over the plate as far as an off-speed pitch. He had a great one. When you make a hitter buckle a little bit, you have a good curve ball."

When Brett stepped into the box, he should have immediately noticed a game of musical chairs that had broken out in the middle of the infield. In addition to the insertion of pitcher Martinez, second-sacker Dauer had slipped over to third base. Belanger moved into his familiar role as shortstop and Garcia slipped over to fill the vacancy at second.

It didn't matter to the game's best batsman. Brett took a Martinez pitch the other way for his first hit of the game. Royals catcher Darrell Porter had never been tied down to the base paths. Coming off a brilliant 1979 season in which he finished second in the league in on-base percentage (.421) and legged out 10 three-baggers, this was a dangerous spot in Stone's bid for his 13th victory. Porter hit the ball directly at the game's new second baseman. Garcia didn't blow his opportunity and got two outs on this play, doubling up Brett.

Martinez surrendered a walk to Willie Mays Aikens and ended the frame when Otis flied out.

The Royals would win 92 games and represent the junior circuit in the World Series. They did not go gently into the night. U.L.Washington's one-out single in the ninth made the 26-year-old shortstop the tying run. Weaver had seen enough, and he summoned Big Foot into the game. Tim Stoddard's first batter was the fleet-footed Wilson. The outfielder would lead the league in at-bats (705) and base hits (230) while finishing fourth in league MVP voting. But he wasn't so dangerous on this night. He bounced one right back at Stoddard, who took the easy out at first. Both runners moved into scoring position. Designated hitter Hal McRae had batted .455 a decade earlier in the 1970 World Series, although his Reds lost the battle with the powerful Birds. Garcia was again called on. The 4-3 out ended the contest. Stoddard's 12th save was in the book.

"We were a pretty good team," Stoddard said. "It takes your role players to put your over the top. It's that extra guy. That third, fourth or fifth pitcher. You just don't plan on him having that type of year. He would be penciled in for 10 or 11 wins. He ended up having a tremendous year. I recall we scored a lot of runs for him. If the other team would score one, we would come back with two."

The shortest pitcher on the O's staff was clearly its best pitcher right now.

"I'm a shade under 5-10," Stone told the *Times*. "Every manager who ever looked at me said, 'Well, maybe he could start 10 or 12 times but he's not durable enough to pitch a whole season.' There are a whole lot of people out there telling you you can't do things. They put restrictions on you. I was starting to believe I couldn't be a starting pitcher a whole year. The worst thing that can happen is for you to start believing the tags they put on you."

Outfielder Dan Ford felt Stone had made a complete overhaul of his pitching plans.

"He changed his philosophy of pitching," Ford said. "Being a little more in control of his pitches and knowing your hitters and situations of that nature. It must be thinking about the whole game of baseball while on the mound. You've got the ball in your hands. You are the controller."

It was the halfway point in the Major League schedule. With Stone's 13th win of the season, the Birds were seven games up on mediocrity. Still, the 44-37 mark was only good for third place, two games back of Milwaukee and nine full games behind New York. And the damn Yanks didn't seem to lose.

John's complete-game shutout on Saturday over his former employer from Chicago gave him a record identical (13-3) to Stone's. In Oakland, Norris also chalked up another victory with a little help. Left-handed reliever Craig Minetto, who would record a 7.88 season ERA in 1980, caught Rod Carew looking at a called third strike for the final out in a 5-4 Oakland win. Norris was now 11-6. He led his league in innings pitched (153) and strikeouts (99) and was second in ERA (2.53).

When KC lefty Gura beat the Orioles' Mike Flanagan on July 27, he, too, was an 11-game winner.

"I'm conditioned for it because of the conditioning program I'm on," Gura told the AP. "I may not throw as hard but I want to be as strong in the ninth inning as I am in the first. Baseball players are about the worst conditioned athletes around. We train hard in the spring but after the season starts, we hardly do anything. By the end of the season, a lot of guys are tired."

On Bastille Day, July 14, some odd things happened. Eight-time Gold Glover Mark Belanger booted two balls on this night. McGregor, in his first attempt at 10 wins, instead surrendered 11 base knocks in less than five innings of work. Kansas City doubled up the Orioles, 8-4. At Comiskey, the runaway Yanks spotted the Chisox six runs in the first three frames. The Yanks chipped away and closed in for the kill. The 7-6 victory pushed the O's 11 games back. Since the calendar opened to the month of May, the Yanks had showed the world it was their turn. By winning 46 and dropping just 19, the Yankees gave Orioles fans other options for their summer vacations. Even with eight Yanks-Orioles games remaining on the schedule, easy mathematics suggested that a pennat race was not likely in this division. And only another Mike Torrez loss kept Baltimore out of fifth place in the American League. Detroit was now in third. On Tuesday, July 15, the O's headed to Milwaukee. Stone was scheduled to hurl the middle game of the three-game series.

The second-place Brewers didn't lose any ground to New York on Tuesday night. Standing 8.5 games back of the leaders, Milwaukee (48-38) trotted out 31-year-old southpaw Mike Caldwell. Two years earlier, he ran second to Guidry in the Cy Young voting with his marvelous 22-9 campaign, highlighted by his Major League-high 23 complete games. Even on a Wednesday evening, close to 32,000 fans arrived at County Stadium to see Caldwell battle the American League's hottest pitcher. Catcher Rick Dempsey was three seasons shy of his MVP performance in the 1983 World Series. But at 31 years old, the former Yankee hit a career high .262 in 1980. Since Stone's winning streak took foot in early May, Dempsey had put on the mask 7 of the 11 times Stone took the hill.

"Dempsey was terrific for me," Stone said. "He could catch it and throw it. He was outstanding. He would say, 'Unless you throw it over my head, it won't get by me.' I give Rick a lot of credit. If you have confidence in your catcher that's great. If you don't trust your catcher, you are in trouble."

Dempsey hit .237 when catching Stone and clearly was not the offensive threat that the lefty-swinger Graham was. Except on this night against Caldwell. After the first six batters pounded the ball into the ground for easy outs to open the contest, Ayala's two-bagger opened up the visitor's second. Ayala, the O's designated hitter, got some early exercise when Dempsey drove him and Roenicke home with another double. It was 3-0 Birds.

Stone finally broke the mold on ground balls to his infielders when he closed the perfect second frame with a strikeout of Sixto Lezcano. The next time Lezcano came up to bat, there were two runners on and one runner home in the fourth inning. He struck out again and Stone and the Birds clung to a 3-1 advantage. By the sixth, the lead had doubled. Dempsey's fifth home run of the season chased both Roenicke and DeCinces home, and for that matter, Caldwell to the showers.

Teammate Lary Sorensen could feel for the southpaw.

"It's frustrating for Mike," Sorensen told the *Journal.* "It's bothering him. We talked about it in the clubhouse. When he struck out Lee May, I said, 'Damn, that's him. He's going to shut them out the rest of the way.' Then they scored three runs."

Cecil Cooper touched Stone for a solo shot in the home half of the sixth. This was the third long ball Stone had surrendered to Cooper in the past two series. It also gave the southpaw slugger the distinction of hitting more homers (five) off of Stone than any other player in the big leagues. Roenicke answered back with his third long ball of the season, a two-run shot in the seventh. Stone and the O's were soaring, 8-2. Stone would record one out in the eighth before Tippy Martinez and Sammy Stewart closed the affair, a 10-4 victory.

Stone had breezed to his 12th straight victory and, along with Philadelphia's Steve Carlton, led the Majors in victories (14).

"My teammates have hit well for me," Stone told the *Milwaukee Journal*. "And they have played defense well for me. Look at tonight. They scored 10 runs for me. Doug DeCinces made two nice plays at third and Rich Dauer made a good play at second. Plus, I'm getting a chance to go out there every fourth or fifth day and battle. I just made up my mind at the All-Star break last season that I was going to do the job. I was determined to do what it took to become a successful starting pitcher. I'm not an overpowering pitcher. I have to think a lot and work hard at it. And it's been paying off."

With the winning streak at exactly a dozen games, Stone made a point of passing out compliments to the men around him. Leading the pack was pitching coach Ray Miller.

"He's helped me more than any pitching coach I've ever had," Stone said in the *Milwaukee Journal*.

Miller made some adjustments in Stone's game plan during the two-week stretch in May when he registered three straight no-decisions.

"I just told him to speed up his delivery between pitches to develop a rhythm," Miller said. "Then I told him not to worry about getting all four of his pitches over the plate in the first inning. When Steve joined our club last season, I think he was trying too much to be something he wasn't — an overpowering pitcher. Now, he concentrates on getting his curveball over for strikes and it's making his fastball more effective."

Miller noted the winning had not gone to Stone's head.

"Steve is a classy guy," he said. "After he was picked for the All-Star team, he sent everyone on the club a thank-you note. He realizes that it takes more than good pitching for a pitcher to put together the kind of winning streak that he has going."

Two starts removed from his heroics in the All-Star Game, Stone could sit back and reflect on his accomplishments that night in Los Angeles.

"That was the highlight of my career," Stone said. "No doubt about it. I've never felt better walking off the mound. It was great."

In New York, it rained. And then it let up. It began raining hits in the home half of the third. Six singles and a Bob Watson triple helped the Yanks put a seven-spot on the board. Tom Underwood and the first-place Yanks enjoyed an 11-1 laugher. Obviously, Stone wasn't pitching during Thursday's matinee in Milwaukee. So the Orioles hitters took the day off. In search of his 10th win, 27-year-old southpaw, Billy Travers went the distance.

He surrendered only a Garcia single and a two-out second inning solo homer by DeCinces. The O's third baseman received a game-winning hit for his seventh blast of the season. Dennis Martinez allowed three hits to Gorman Thomas alone but pitched scoreless ball until two outs in the ninth. Tippy Martinez (no relation) induced Ben Oglivie to bounce to Dauer with two on for the game's final out in a 1-0 decision. In the Bronx that evening, the left-hander John was afforded the opportunity to tie Stone for the league lead in victories. The first two Twins reached base and John was down a run heading to the home team's first at-bats. By the second, he could stop worrying. Lou Pinella, who batted exactly once for the 1964 Orioles, singled in a pair as the Yanks scored four times off Geoff Zahn. John went the distance and fanned just one in a 10-3 romp.

"No chance," barked Minnesota manager Gene Mauch to a reporter inquiring whether any team could actually catch the Yankees. "Just forget it. They probably have the best pitching the Yankees have had since Whitey Ford was a little kid pitching with (Allie) Reynolds, (Vic) Raschi and (Eddie) Lopat. And they have depth on their bench. Those guys come to the ballpark every night feeling they're going to win."

The Yankees were now winning two of every three games and the 57-29 mark was the best in baseball. The O's could take some solace in the fact that the wins over the Brewers had created a tie with Milwaukee in second place in the loss column.

On Friday night, July 18, Kansas City's Gura and Oakland's Norris were slated for starts. Actually both pitchers had enough run support on this night for a few starts.

Gura's run support came in Yankee Stadium and he and the visitors gave the New Yorkers a taste of what the postseason would be like. Gura needed only one run as he spotted the Majors' best team just three hits and no earned runs in sailing through a complete game. The left-hander was 14-3 and comfortably ahead in the ERA race with a sporty 2.09. Willie Wilson had four singles and a double. George Brett contributed three singles and his ninth homer. Amos Otis settled for four singles in a 13-1 demolition before 44,000 stunned New Yorkers. There were fewer than 6,000 in Oakland to watch the A's play long ball.

Tony Armas and Mitchell Page each hit a pair of homers as Norris had eight runs to work with by the fifth. He sailed home to his 12th win of the season, 9-1 over the visiting Indians. Norris stood second to Gura for the league lead in ERA (2.44). This twosome was also one -two in the AL in innings pitched.

On Monday, July 21, the Orioles took a 5-1 lead to the third inning in Minnesota.Pete Mackanin laced an 11th inning single off loser Tippy Martinez as the Twins took gameone of a twin bill 8-7. You couldn't really blame Tippy as he was on his fifth inning of relief. Six Orioles hitters had two hits as the O's wasted a 15-hit attack. Stone and his dozen-game win streak was ready for game two of the doubleheader. And so was his favorite left-handed hitting backstop. Graham never seemed to let the Twins forget he was their fifth pick in the 1975 amateur draft.

The short-lived phrase "Dan Graham Grand Slam" was coined on this night in the Twin Cities. Before his hitting heroics were noted, the O's catcher showed off his defensive skills. Well, sort of. Rob Wilfong was the first baserunner of the game as the Twins second sacker reached on Graham's interference. Wilfong tested the arm of the allegedly shaken Graham. He was gunned down. Stone took matters into his own hands in the third.

Mackanin went down on strikes. Ron Jackson repeated that performance. And catcher Sal Butera completed the trifecta as Stone whiffed the side in order. By the second time around the order, the Birds had figured out Twins lefty Geoff Zahn. Graham didn't flinch against the southpaw and his grand slam decided this contest early. In game No. 91, it was the O's first grand slam of the season. Lee May homered in the fifth and it was 6-0. Graham added a two-run single in the next frame as the lead doubled. The league's best pitcher was up a dozen runs.

"He pitched occasionally for us in 1979," Singleton said. "But he got on a roll. We scored an awful lot of runs that year for him. It seemed like we had five runs before he took the mound."

It was 12-0 heading to the eighth inning. Three walks loaded the bases for the left-fielder Jackson. His two-bagger cleared the bases and cut Stone's lead to nine runs. Stoddard was called in, and he promptly surrendered two hits and a walk. The margin of safety was now down to seven runs. The 12-5 romp gave Stone the victory he needed to tie for his career-high in victories (15), three seasons earlier in a White Sox uniform.

"The Orioles were very team-oriented," Stoddard said. "There were a lot of great players. He wasn't the main pitcher and that made it a little easier."

Now riding a Major League best 13-game winning streak, the 32-year-old right-hander could look back at 11 seasons as an average pitcher.

"Then, I was hoping for luck instead of making it," Stone told the *Washington Post*. "I'd change my uniform number. Or shave my mustache before I pitched as though I hoped they wouldn't realize it was me out there."

Even pitching for an Orioles club that won 102 games in 1979, Stone finished fouth in the AL in homers allowed (31).

"In the back of my mind, I assumed everything was going to go wrong," Stone added. "I gave up 31 homers last year and it seemed like half of them barely cleared the fence."

On the night of July 21, Stone's record was a gorgeous 15-3.

On Monday, the Brewers had 17 hits versus Yankees pitching. On Tuesday night, they had one Buck Martinez single heading to the seventh inning. It was Tommy John's turn in the Yanks rotation. He walked just one and fanned only two but the result was a 4-hit whitewash of the Brew-Crew. John was very much in the hunt for the Cy Young hardware. The 37-year-old lefty joined Stone in the 15-3 club.

"There is no pressure there," John told the AP. "When you face a team like the Brewers, you just hope you can go out and pitch your best. When you're a veteran ballclub, the pressure is on the clubs behind you, not on you. We are a very confident ball club."

July 22 marked an 8-4 win by Flanagan and the Orioles over the Twins. The former Cy Young Award winner sat down with Stone prior to this winning performance.

"That was the best curve ball I've had all year," Flanagan told the AP. "I talked to Steve and he told me a couple of things to look for. Tonight, they were swinging at the curve and missing so that was a good sign."

Another half game was chopped off the Yanks' lead. Twin bills were popular on this Tuesday. The Jays and A's split a pair in Oakland. Norris was on the mound in game two for Oakland. He tossed a four-hit shutout and complete game earned him his 13th win of the season. Norris was now second to Gura in ERA (2.37) and led the league in strikeouts (109) after fanning six Blue Jays. On Wednesday,

Guidry threw another four-hitter at the Brewers. The lefty won his 11th game and regained the AL lead in strikeouts.

Meanwhile, Gura was at home versus the White Sox. U.L. Washington homered in the opening frame to give Gura the early lead. Washington's blast represented one-sixth of his long ball production during a campaign in which he came to the plate more than 600 times. Losing pitcher Ross Baumgarten lasted only one inning. He also had an inkling before the contest that it would be a difficult assignment to stop Gura and the Royals.

"Good, bring him on," Baumgarten said to the *Chicago Tribune*. "But I'll probably have to pitch a shutout to win."

Gura went seven solid innings for his 13th win versus four defeats. Kansas City won going away, 9-2. His ERA slipped to 2.11, which was tops in the American League. On July 23, Stone had the longest winning streak in Majors. He was tied for the league lead in wins (15). But his competitors were taking top honors in more than one category. John had those 15 wins to go with a league-high six shutouts. Gura was third in wins (13), second in innings pitched (170) and held tightly to the ERA lead. Norris was second in punchouts (109) and ERA (2.37). He was tops in innings hurled (171) and third in complete games (14). And unlike both John and Gura, Stone's team was not in the hunt. Little did anyone guess, Baltimore would finish the season winning 49 of its last 69 games (.710).

Also on July 23, McGregor reached double figures in victories when he survived a rocky first inning at the Met in Minnesota. Singleton had a four-hit night in the 8-7 win. Graham continued his punishment of his former employer with a three-RBI night. Trailing the third-place Brewers by a scant half game, the O's headed home for a weekend series with Milwaukee. Stone was scheduled to pitch the middle game of the three-game set.

Reggie Cleveland would throw the final two shutouts of his 13-year career in 1980. One of them came in Memorial Stadium on Friday, July 25. During his complete-game four hitter, no O's player reached third base. Palmer took the 5-0 loss. That same night 40,000 packed into Royals Stadium to see Clint Hurdle's inside-the-park homer help the home team topple the Yanks 6-1.

The Stone-Caldwell rematch brought in 31,000 on Saturday night. Hall-of-Famer Paul Molitor had 20 or more doubles in 17 different seasons. On this night, he immediately put Stone into hot water, going the opposite way with the leadoff two-bagger. With one out, Molitor swiped third base. With Molitor 90 feet away, Cecil Cooper hit the ball up the middle, but Stone snared it and caught Molitor in no-man's land. A short rundown ensued, and the Milwaukee second baseman was toast when DeCinces tagged him out. Catcher Dempsey batted second on this night and ended the O's scoring drought with a solo homer, his sixth of the campaign. He would also make contributions in the field as well.

"Rick was exceptional," Stone told the *Sun.*

Both pitchers settled down to business entering the fourth inning. But this was a Brewers offense that didn't remain quiet for long. At season's end, the club from Milwaukee had three members with 100 or more RBI. Leading the pack with 122 was the stylish Cecil Cooper. He pushed a hit to right to open the fourth. Gorman Thomas (105 RBI in 1980) launched a ground-rule double. The visitors had runners on second and third with no outs. This is where Stone got some help from backstop Dempsey. Where Cooper was going was anyone's guess. What mattered is the 30-year-old superstar was caught dreaming as he opened up his lead towards home. Dempsey picked him off for a huge out.

"When Dempsey picked that runner off with men on third and second and nobody out, it was a tremendous lift," Stone said, according to the *Sun.*

"We had our chances tonight," Brewers manager George Bamberger told the hometown *Milwaukee Journal.* "We had the men there and couldn't do anything. We ran the bases bad."

Dempsey struck again in the fifth inning. After Jim Gantner singled with one out and then broke for second base.. Dempsey fired a strike to shortstop Garcia and the threat was over.

Molitor led off the sixth inning as well. He didn't risk getting snared in Dempsey's trap. Molitor hit only nine homers this season. But his fifth blast of the campaign tied this affair up at 1-1. Robin Yount singled and stole a base in this frame, but Stone escaped unscathed. Dempsey rose up again in the visitor's seventh. Charlie Moore singled with two outs. He, too, tested Dempsey's throwing arm. He, too, retreated to the bench when he was caught stealing for the third out. After two were out in the O's half of the frame, Murray, batting right-handed, took a chunk out of the left field wall with a booming two-bagger. Designated hitter Ayala had not put a ball out of the infield in two previous at-bats versus Caldwell. But this was 1980, the only season of his 10-year career in which the platoon player hit double figures in homers. Ayala cracked one to left-center, and Stone and the O's were up 3-1. It was the 29-year-old's seventh homer of the year.

Reached at his home in Puerto Rico, Ayala had fond memories of Stone's remarkable campaign.

"He was a single person and he took vitamins," Ayala said. "He took care of himself. His nickname was Pebbles. He had those broad shoulders. He would pitch in those Orange uniforms. It gave him a different feeling. It was a positive feeling."

Yount ripped a one-out double in the eighth, one of his league-leading 49 two-baggers.

Stone then threw one that hit Cooper, and the Brew-Crew was in business again with runners on first and second. Thomas was the third member of his team with 100 or more RBI (105). He was also third in the league in homers (38). He also led the league in free-swinging and fanned a league-worst 170 times. He didn't miss a Stone offering. Thomas' high drive leaped towards the left field foul pole. There was no doubt it had the distance for a three-run homer.

However, it slipped all of two feet foul of the fair pole. It was a very long strike.

Manager Weaver evidently gulped and reached for his cavalry, calling Stoddard's number to finish Thomas' at-bat. Thomas connected with a drive to left for a single, but at least the ball stayed in the ballpark. Yount did not test the arm of Roenicke and the sacks were loaded for the always dangerous Ben Ogilive. The 31-year-old slugger had his best season in 1980. Stoddard had to face a player who would lead the league in homers (41). He was second in total bases (331), and second in RBI (118). In close to 600 at-bats, the selective power hitter fanned only 71 times. Stone's winning streak was on the line when Stoddard faced Ogilvie with the sacks loaded.

"I got to know Steve pretty well," Stoddard said. "He ended up living in the area. We would see each other at area functions. He was a veteran who knew how to get in shape. He was that type of player who knew what his strengths were. There was no doubt Steve was the fourth or fifth starter at the beginning of the season. He was a fastball-power pitcher to begin his career. He became more of a finesse pitcher when he got older."

Stoddard was anything but a finesse pitcher. He threw smoke. Ogilvie may have solved *New York Times* puzzles, but he couldn't catch up with a Stoddard blazer and fanned for the second out. Dick Davis pushed one to Dauer at second and the O's lead — and Stone's winning streak — was safe for another inning. With Stone still eligible for his 14th consecutive victory, DeCinces led off the eighth with his eighth homer of the season. It was 4-1. The Brewers went quietly in the ninth, and Stone secured his career-high 16th win. The 14-game winning streak was now part of Orioles history.

"In back to back games with Milwaukee, I threw something like 74 and 77 curveballs," Stone told this writer. "I threw a lot of curveballs at different speeds and different angles. My best one was about 68 miles per hour and it was a little looper. It used to drive hitters crazy. They were able to guess it was a curveball, but they couldn't guess the speed. You might even guess the velocity but it's harder whether it's up or down and three different speeds. My curve was as good as anyone's that year. I always had a good curveball."

After securing his 16th victory, Stone commented about his winning streak.

"I really don't think about the streak," Stone told the *Journal.* "People say there must be tremendous pressure. I don't even think about it. Tonight, I wasn't thinking about it at all. I was thinking about winning my 16th game. Now, I'll be thinking about No. 17 instead of winning 15 in a row."

His 14-game winning streak was the Majors' longest since the 1974 season. On opening day that season, the Yankees handled Cleveland's Gaylord Perry 6-1. On July 3rd, Perry beat the Brewers 4-3 to move to 15-1. Unlike Stone, Perry went the other way as a 10-inning defeat to Vida Blue and the defending World Champion A's ignited a personal five-game losing streak.

Perry would finish 21-13.

Stone was in the company of some great hurlers. Walter "Big Train" Johnson and Smoky Joe Wood each won 16 consecutive games in 1912. Nineteen years later, Philadelphia's Lefty Grove matched that record. His 16 straight victories helped pave the way to a 31-victory campaign. The Major League record pre-dated World War I. Both Tim Keefe and Rube Marquardt notched 19 consecutive wins. Of course, Stone was also short of the Orioles record. Dave McNally, dubbed "Dave McLucky," opened the 1969 season by winning 15 straight contests. It took a pinch-hit grand slam homer from southpaw swinging Rich Reese to help the Twins end McNally's string of victories in early August of that season. The late Orioles star, too, tumbled a bit late in the campaign of 1969. His mark was 5-7 after the great start.

The 1977 AL Cy Young Award went to a Yankees reliever. During the regular season, southpaw Albert Walter Lyle won or saved 39 percent of all of New York's victories. Sparky Lyle's Yanks won the World Series. Three years later, he was pitching in relief for Texas.

His replacement, Richard Michael Gossage, couldn't match that 39 percent in 1980, but he would settle for six wins and 33 saves (37.8 percent). After making 29 starts for the 1976 White Sox, Gossage turned the page on his career and completed it making the next 814 appearances as a reliever as one of the fiercest game-finishers in the game's history.

On the night Stone won his 14th straight game, Gossage also added to a streak. Reggie Jackson's league-leading 28th homer of the season provided the difference as Goose Gossage ran his record to 4-0 with a 5-4 win over KC.

"He's all arms and legs," Yankees first baseman Bob Watson said, describing Gossage to the *New York Times*. "And he's not looking at you. That doesn't make you feel good when he's throwing 100 miles per hour. I don't mind a guy throwing 100 miles per hour if he's look-ing at you. I'll tell you it's a lot better playing behind him."

On the last day of June, Gossage earned a save in Tommy John's 11th win of the season. Red Sox slugger Tony Perez never had a chance.

"Bang, bang, bang," Yankees catcher Rick Cerone told the *Times*. "Harder, harder, harder. And all on the outside corner. Those were his best three fastballs of the year."

"There is no way in the world I could have hit those three pitches," said Perez, whose strikeout came with the bases loaded.

Before his blistering fastball headed towards the plate, opposing hitters were treated to a flying body show.

"He has the strength," Pirates manager ChuckTanner told the *Times*. "He also had the proper mental makeup. If someone got a hit off him, he'd get so ticked, he want to throw the ball through the backstop. A young man who threw as hard as he did, I just knew he'd make an excellent relief pitcher."

Tanner, who came to Pittsburgh from Chicago, was the manager who converted Gossage into one of history's best closers.

Gossage was well aware he had something good going.

"For a hitter, I think the way I throw makes the ball tougher to see than for 80 to 90 percent of the other pitchers," Gossage told the *Times*. "I rear back and they see a lot of butt, arms, and legs coming at them. It's tough."

Kansas City was the spot to be on Sunday night, July 27. For the first-place Royals, 14-game winner, Gura looked to improve his record. For the visiting Yankees, also a first-place club, 15-game winner John took the hill. More than 40,000 came out this night to see the two best southpaws in the league go at it. John was riding a modest four-game win streak.

Gura's no-hit bid died on the first batter of the night as Willie Randolph went up the middle for his safety. That was about the extent of the excitement for the visitors from the Bronx. John exited in the fourth after the Royals fell one homer short of a cycle in the six-run frame. Gura easily pocketed win No. 15 in the 8-0 smashing. In addition, the Kansas City ace took over the league lead in ERA (2.01). That same night, two left-handers also squared off in Baltimore. These southpaws, Flanagan for the Orioles and Billy Travers for the Brewers, combined to surrender 19 hits in 15 innings of work. Relievers Stoddard and Bob McClure were considerably less generous. In a combined eight innings of action, those two hurlers allowed just three hits together. The Brewers held a 4-1 lead in the eighth, but Ayala's two-run blast closed the gap. A Lenn Sakata sacrifice fly scored DeCinces later in the inning to tie the game. It went a dozen innings before pinch-hitter Lowenstein's liner to center skipped by Gorman Thomas producing the 53rd win of the season. In the process, the O's also slipped right by the Brewers and into third place, eight games back.

On Tuesday the 27th the Orioles moved into second place for the first time since April 20. Roenicke's solo homer in the eighth gave Scott McGregor and the O's a 4-0 lead in Texas. That looked to be enough to give the southpaw his 11th win of the season. And it was-barely enough. The Rangers scored three times in the ninth and moved the tying run to second base. Tippy Martinez relieved Stoddard and retired Richie Zisk to end the uprising. And the script played out from there. The Tigers gave up two homers to former O's star Bobby Grich and were otherwise toothless in a 7-0 loss to California. And in Minnesota, light-hitting Rob Wilfong did his part to ignite a pennant chase in the AL East. Loser Luis Tiant excused Kenny Landreaux from batting in the eighth and loaded the bases after the intentional pass. Wilfong foiled that by knocking in a pair with a hit up the middle. The visiting Yanks crawled within a single run in the ninth but starter Geoff Zahn completed his 10-hitter in the 3-2 win.

The Yanks lead was slimmed to 7½ games over the second-place Birds. Less than 24 hours later, the lead dropped another game.

On Wednesday night in Arlington, the two men pitching for their respective clubs had combined for 520 major league victories. Gaylord Perry was 41-years-old and didn't know it at the time but was to be thrust into the middle of the Orioles-Yankees AL East race within a few weeks. His opponent, Jim Palmer, was beginning to eat up some innings in support of Stone and his teammates.

A pair of doubles off the bats of Graham and Murray gave Palmer a quick 2-0 lead.

Bump Wills cut the lead in half with an inside-the-park homer. Bumbry's seventh inning two-bagger proved to be the difference in a 3-2 decision.

That night at the Met, ex-Met Jerry Koosman was spinning some magic at the visiting Yanks. Willie Randolph, Rupert Jones, Reggie Jackson and Lou Piniella combined on an 0--for-16 night. Twins third baseman John Castino was the reigning American League Rookie of the Year. On this late July evening, he had four hits. He followed up Landreaux's infield hit with a double to right with two outs in the 10th. That game-winning safety registered defeat No. 1 of the campaign on the fireballer Gossage's record. New York had dropped two in a row in Minnesota.To find a longer losing streak on the Yanks' schedule, one would have to drift back to mid-April.

Gossage didn't wait around to sulk about his first defeat. Thursday night at County Stadium featured a battle of lefties, John for New York and Caldwell for Milwaukee. It was 2-1 Brewers until the seventh. That's when Yount doubled home two,and Cooper homered in two. John and teammates were staring at consecutive loss No. 3 with two at-bats left and a five-run deficit. Reggie Jackson ignored the lefty-lefty matchup presented by Bob McClure and launched his 29th homer of the season to knot this game at 6-6. The three-run blast also took John off the hook. Gossage earned his 5th win of the campaign, a 7-6 decision. The right-hander went 3 innings of the 11 played that night.

July 31, 1980

American League East	W	L	Pct.	GB
New York	62	37	.626	—
Baltimore	55	43	.561	6½
Milwaukee	54	45	.545	8
Detroit	51	44	.537	9
Cleveland	49	47	.510	11½
Boston	50	48	.510	11½
Toronto	43	55	.439	18½

Pitching Matchup

Baltimore (Steve Stone 16-3, 3.09) at Texas (Ferguson Jenkins 9-9, 3.53)

14

End of the line

In Arlington, Baltimore's Stone was out chasing history again. He had already topped veteran Fergie Jenkins in mid-May. The rematch would be on Thursday night. Texas first baseman Pat Putnam batted sixth in this contest. And the left-handed hitter took a called third strike in the opening inning. That was only significant because that was the first Texas hitter retired. There were no doubles, triples or homers hit in this frame but four singles and an infield error. The league's best pitcher had been hit with a four- spot. Dan Graham's catcher's interference and Kiko Garcia's boot at short made half the runs unearned. But the bid to extend the 14-game winning streak was off to a rocky start.

"For some reason we always seem to do great against Mr. Stone," said Texas manager Pat Corrales in the *Dallas Morning News*. "He's usually just a five- or six-inning pitcher against us."

In the third, Stone's old nemesis, John Grubb, singled, stole a base, jumped to third on the error by Graham, and came home on

Jim Sundberg's single. It was 5-0 Texas. When Mickey Rivers opened inning No. 4 with a two-bagger, Weaver strolled to the mound and took Stone out of the game. Reliever Dennis Martinez surrendered two more hits in the frame, and it was ugly: Texas 7, Baltimore 0. It was Stone's shortest stint since the six-run first on April 25.

Roenicke opened the fifth inning and spoiled Jenkins' bid for a shutout. It was his fifth homer of the campaign. Pat Kelly's single chased home Singleton in the sixth and the deficit was now five runs at 7-2. It stayed that way until the ninth. Singleton's two-out hit drove in two, and the tying run strolled to the dish in the person of Eddie Murray. Right-hander Danny Darwin would finish 171 games during his 21-year campaign. That's the same number of games he won. He set a career high for saves (8) during his 13-win season. Darwin retired Murray on a roller to third and the 14-game winning streak was no more.

"The streak was of no consequence to me," Stone told the *News*. "We got in a groove, and the team played very well behind me. It's impossible to look at tonight and complain. I've been so fortunate over this whole streak. Tonight was a combination at least for three innings of nobody having a very good night, certainly including me. But they've supported me so well this was bound to happen sometime. I'm sitting here with a 16-4 record. We won two of three games from a team that can hit like this one can. And I'll win No. 17 Tuesday night. I'm happy."

Stone had not tasted defeat since the May 5.

"There was never any pressure," Stone told the AP. "I didn't think about it that much. I thought I threw pretty decently. I've won with worse stuff."

The longest winning streak in the Majors had closed. And it gave the right-hander some moments to ponder what he had accomplished.

"I knew it was coming," Stone told the *Chicago Tribune*. "I said so in the middle of last season. I said the only thing between me and an exceptional year was not having the chance to have it. It was a whole transformation. I was as strong as I've ever been physically, and I was mentally prepared to do the job. But I knew I couldn't do it out of the fifth starter's spot. I told the reporters in spring training I was going to win 18 games this year. Since the most I had ever won was 15, and that was only once, they didn't believe me."

With a 16-4 record, Stone was in no way sulking about this latest loss. He was still along for the ride of his life.

"I've always loved to talk," Stone said. "Now I've found somebody to listen. Sure, I could be bitter about it. I could say where were you guys two years ago? I'm not any smarter now or wittier. But there's too much bitterness in the world already. If I can't make myself happy with this type of season I might as well retire because they're not going to get any better.

"I've tried to enjoy every minute of it," he added. "Vin Scully said it very well at the All-Star game luncheon. He said, 'In the twinkling of an eyelash you go from the All-Star Game to an old-timers game.' Things that were once out of the question are happening daily," Stone said. "It's all pretty nice."

As play closed on the first day of August, there were exactly two pennant chases alive and well in Major League play. And both belonged to the National League. After exactly 100 games, the Montreal Expos and Pittsburgh Pirates each had 45 losses. The Phillies had one more defeat. The National League West was playing a similar tune. Houston was the team with 45 losses. The Dodgers stood one game back in the loss column.

The AL West was in shambles. The only excitement was Brett's chase of the elusive .400 mark. He stood at an impressive .388. His team was a dozen games up. The Orioles were clearly playing better. With a 17-9 mark in June followed by a 16-11 record in July, the O's had cruised into second place. Stone and the pitching staff had surrendered the fewest runs in the league (406). The daunting Yankees lead was still 7.5 games, however. The one glimmer of hope was these two clubs had eight meetings scheduled for the month of August. And that's exactly when the Orioles would have to make their move. These two powers would play on Aug. 18 and never see each other again the rest of the way.

The Chicago White Sox simply weren't hitting. In its previous 13 games, the Sox had averaged just over 3.5 runs a game. That's one important reason why Chicago stood nine games under the .500 mark and 17.5 games off the pace in the AL West. On Tuesday night, Stone's mound opponent would be the rookie La Marr Hoyt. Drafted by the Yankees in the fifth round of the 1973 draft, he was tossed into the 1977 deal that sent Bucky Dent to New York. There was that one memorable homer for Dent in 1978 versus 74 wins and the 1983 American League Cy Young Award in five seasons for Hoyt. And, the White Sox later dealt Hoyt to San Diego for a young shortstop named Ozzie Guillen.

Stone had gone 76 calendar days without a defeat before he was ambushed in Texas. With two out in the first and a runner on third, Stone faced the old Orioles nemesis, Lamar Johnson. The 29-year-old first baseman carried a personal 20-game hit streak against the Orioles alone. And he didn't waste any time switching it to 21 games. Johnson didn't miss a hanging Stone curve and sent it halfway up the bleachers in left.

"It was a pretty good curve," Stone told the *Chicago Tribune.* "Below the knees. He went down and got it. It didn't bother me that much."

It was Johnson's 13th homer of the season. For the season, Johnson managed 22 hits in 46 trips to plate against Orioles pitching, good enough to tie with Tony Perez for the lead in batting average against the 1980 Orioles. Perez, too, went 22-for-46 against Baltimore's hurlers.

The homer was Johnson's fifth of the campaign vs. the Orioles and also his final one for 1980. He didn't launch another long ball the rest of the campaign, and he nailed only eight more homers until he called it quits in 1982.

Stone settled down. He had a 1-2-3 second and steered out of two -on trouble in the third. And his offense was trying to come back against the hard-throwing Hoyt.

"He (Hoyt) has very good stuff," said O's designated hitter Terry Crowley. "He threw three or four different pitches and every one of them is a big league pitch. It seemed like he got them all over for strikes, too."

Of course it didn't help that one O's base runner fell asleep. Garcia, Bumbry, Dauer and Murray all laced singles against Hoyt in the third inning. The windfall was a single run. Bumbry held up on Murray's clean hit. That was fine but there were two outs and the speedster should have been in the dugout looking for a quick snack. Hoyt and the Sox led 2-1. Both Crowley and Garcia were strikeout victims in the fourth. Designated hitter Bobby Molinaro had his second hit off Stone in the fifth but was thrown out trying for the extra base.

The O's fifth decided this contest. Bumbry again had base-running problems. Hoyt had Bumbry picked off, only to see Johnson fire the ball away and move Bumbry up a bag. It was contagious. Shortstop Todd Cruz kicked away a Singleton grounder. Lowenstein made the Sox pay with a game-tying hit. And Crowley decided this contest with one swing of his bat. Stone now had a 4-run lead to work with. The King of Swing had cleaned the bags with a grand slam.

"I had to fight off some real tough pitches," he said. "And hope he got one over that I could hit. Even the one I hit he made a nice pitch on it. It was a changeup and it was down and it was a strike. You can't ask him to do more than that. I just got lucky on it."

Stone allowed another Johnson hit in the sixth but escaped further damage. Dauer scored Bumbry in the home half of the sixth and it was 7-2. Stone had a 1-2-3 seventh and then let Dennis Martinez get in some work.

"I was just a little tired," Stone said that night. "And the innings and the two starts are beginning to pile up. And I'm going to face the Yankees in three days. I didn't think I had very good stuff tonight. Ironically, I had better stuff against Texas and I lost with it. I knew the White Sox were going to get more hits than usual tonight. I just didn't want to put anyone on base ahead of them, especially Lamar Johnson."

Weaver noted his ace was laboring in the seventh inning.

"He said he was stiffening up pretty good," Weaver told the *Sun*. "And it looked like he was out of steam, too. He was going to go out for the eighth but then I changed my mind."

DeCinces homered off the left field foul pole notching the final run of the game. Stone moved to 17-4 with the 8-2 decision. Again, run support was key.

"It's just positive thinking," Stone said. "And eight runs a game. Never underestimate the importance of eight runs a game."

Weaver was well aware there weren't many pitchers in the AL who could match Stone in the confidence game.

"That 14-game winning streak got Steve's confidence as high as it can get," Weaver said. "It can't get no higher."

Only Stone's loss to Texas separated the O's from a 10-game winning streak. The Yanks lead had slipped to six full games and just five in the all-knowing loss column. Two more home games with the Sox remained before the O's would head north for a three-game series in the Bronx.

It wasn't too early to peek ahead. Game one on Friday night would feature four of the Cy Young Award winners of the 1970s. Palmer took the bulk of that with the plaques in 1973, 1975 and 1976. Guidry's brilliant 1978 season featured a 25-3 mark with a dazzling 1.74 ERA. Stone would take the mound on Saturday night, Aug. 9.

His mound foe would be a 1972 second-round pick of the Phillies. Tom Underwood would win a career-high 13 games during this season. The two southpaws, Flanagan and John would close the three-game series on Sunday.

August 9, 1980

American League East	W	L	Pct.	GB
New York	67	40	.626	—
Baltimore	62	44	.585	4½
Detroit	57	47	.548	8½
Milwaukee	57	51	.528	10½
Boston	56	51	.523	11
Cleveland	54	50	.519	11½
Toronto	45	62	.421	22

Pitching Matchup

Baltimore (Steve Stone 17-4, 3.18) at New York (Tom Underwood 9-7, 4.22)

15
Heavyweights tangle

The stage was set. The Orioles would head to New York with an unblemished mark in the month of August. And since Stone's laugher in Minnesota on July 21, the Birds had taken flight to the tune of 13-2. The league-leading Yankees had dropped back to the pack with an 8-8 mark. Eight games between these two clubs were on tap in the next 10 days. Stone would pitch in two of those contests.

In 1954, the Yankees would win 103 games and post a .668 winning percentage. It wasn't good enough. The upstart Cleveland Indians would win 111 contests and represent the American League in the World Series. That ended a five-year streak in which the Yanks were the champs of the AL every season. Ironically, in winning five straight World Series titles, the Bronx Bombers never won more than 100 games.

Less than 1,000 miles west of the Bronx were the likes of Clint Courtney, Billy Hunter, and Don Larsen riding out a 100-game losing season in the last hurrah of the St. Louis Browns. The next season in

Baltimore, those Browns players would post the exact same mark (54-100). The best team in baseball would meet the new Orioles 22 times in the O's first campaign and pin 17 percent of all the season's defeats on them. It got worse the next season. The Yanks drubbed the O's in 19 of 22 meetings.

But after six straight losing seasons to the New Yorkers, the upstarts from Baltimore began to turn it around. After taking 8 out of 11 meetings in Yankee stadium, the 1959 O's posted a winning record (12-9) head to head. It got much better in a hurry. From 1964-1968, the Orioles handled the Yanks to the tune of 64-26. Entering the 1980 campaign, the Orioles held 246-232 advantage over a team that possessed 32 first-place finishes. The Orioles were the only club in the AL that owned a winning mark against the Yankees. And it would be a hot Orioles club visiting the Bronx for the weekend of Aug 8-10. Since the middle of June, Baltimore had posted a 33-14 mark.

"I don't know anything about momentum," Weaver told the *Times*. "Or any of that stuff. To me it's simple why we're as close as we are. Lately, we've had guys getting the base hit and hitting the home run. Our defense has been good and our pitching has been great. That's the way the American League champions should play and no one should be surprised. We're playing excellent baseball. That's what we're doing. You just can't do any better than we have."

Outfielder Lowenstein sang a similar tune.

"There is no magical ingredient," he told the *Times*. "Baseball success is very basic. If you play well, you're going to win. Good ball clubs with the necessary talent are always terribly optimistic. Clubs with talent, experience and guts will be around when the finish comes and close to the top. It's always the case."

Stone chipped in a few thoughts of his own.

"They've got to be feeling it a little bit," Stone said of the Yanks. "I think the idea of pressure is overrated but every ballclub has a cold period and they haven't hit theirs yet."

Weaver was well aware the Yanks were in no free fall. After 19 victories in both May and June, New York fell just three spots to 16 wins in the month of July.

"We've picked up six in the loss column without the Yankees in a noticeable slump," Weaver said. "Sure, we'd prefer to be in their position but all we have to do is to win five more than they do, no matter who they're against. The only thing is when you spot somebody and they refuse to give in, will there be time to catch them or not?"

Singleton touted the O's pitching staff as the reason the pennant chase was tightening.

"Every night we send a guy out there who's capable of throwing a shutout," he said. "Even when they don't, the guys we bring in are capable of starting for other teams."

Pitching coach Ray Miller was licking his chaps awaiting the series in New York.

"We've been talking about catching them for a month," Miller said. "There won't be anyone here in awe of them. You can count on that. Jeez, I love pennant races. You can have so many feelings in one week. From being on top of the world to lower than dirt. That stuff gets you going whether you admit it or not. That's what it's all about."

With the pitching rotation for the series mapped out, the prospective of a John-Stone engagement went by the wayside. Former O's general manager Harry Dalton weighed in on that subject.

"I'm at the point," Dalton told the *Times*, "where if Stone pitched against John I'd come and see it because one of them would have to lose. And I'd like to see that. If they did pitch against each other they should ballyhoo it like they did in the old days when Bob Feller pitched against Hal Newhouser."

Yankees pitching coach Stan Williams wasn't caught up in that drama.

"We are not going to change our rotation just to get a head-on confrontation," Williams said. "If it happens, it happens."

The New York fans got it. Whether or not the majority thought this would be the three-game series to put away the defending AL champs was not known. But the home that Ruth built was filled on Friday night, Aug. 8. with more than 54,000. For the visitors, the eight-time 20-game winner, 34-year-old Jim Palmer. His mound opponent, Louisiana Lightning, Ron Guidry, less than two years removed from his 25-win campaign of 1978. The O's went 1-2-3 in the first on three ground balls. Bobby Murcer touched Palmer for a safety but his teammates could do nothing with it in the first. Guidry gave free passes to Ayala and Roenicke but Garcia popped up behind the plate with those two aboard in the second.

The Yanks made noise in the third. The first three hitters reached and Murcer's second hit scored Bucky Dent with the game's first run. Reggie Jackson, in his last .300 season in the Majors, looked at strike three and the Bombers settled for one.

Murray broke up any no-hit talk leading off the fourth and DeCinces, a noted Guidry killer, drew a base on balls. This time it was Roenicke fanning with runners on board. Guidry nearly struck out the side in the fifth. Only Bumbry's weak pop-out to Willie Randolph at second spoiled that moment. The O's knotted this tight one in the sixth. Murray and Ayala belted two-out, back-to-back doubles. The Yanks answered with another Jackson strikeout in home half of the inning. The veteran Palmer was sailing. He had retired 11 in a row when former Seattle Mariner Rupert Jones stepped up with two down in the seventh. The seventh-place hitter in manager Dick Howser's lineup sent one out into the night. Jones' eighth homer of the season, (he would add one more the rest of the campaign) gave the home crowd something to scream about. Guidry and possibly Gossage had six outs to go. Murray strolled to the right-handed hitter's batter's box with two outs in the eighth. The future Hall-of-Famer had one double off of Guidry but Howser stuck with the lefty to face the slugger. He paid dearly for it. Murray's 19th homer of the season gave the O's new life. Ayala followed with a hit up the middle. And then Howser traded the DeCinces-Guidry matchup for the fire-balling Gossage-DeCinces, righty-on-righty connection. DeCinces still pulled the Gossage pitch in the direction of left-fielder Murcer.

That's when umpire Durwood Merrill stepped in to make the call. He claimed Murcer trapped DeCinces' two-bagger. The Yanks could not have disagreed more. The captain of the Yankee Clipper, George Steinbrenner, spoke for the troops. Naturally, he was not in atten-dance.

"It's a shame that in a crucial and emotional game in a pennant race that the outcome might be decided by a questionable call. Base-ball men who saw the play tell me that the ball was clearly caught. I just hate to think that the outcome of a pennant race might be de-cided by a questionable call."

The view of this play was decidedly different from the Orioles dugout.

"I don't care what baseball men say," said O's coach Cal Ripken Sr, in the *Baltimore Sun*. "That ball was not caught."

O's owner Edward Bennett Williams agreed with his baseball man's assessment.

"I think Murcer was lucky to trap the ball," Williams told the *Sun*.

DeCinces needed the hit. In his 37 trips to the plate in 1980 ver-sus New York, the third-sacker managed only a .162 mark. With new life, manager Weaver waved in Lowenstein to hit for Roenicke. And when the pinch-hitter delivered, the Birds went up a pair of runs at 4-2. The veteran Palmer smelled blood. Both Willie Randolph and Murcer went down on flies to the outfield. But when Oscar Gamble shot a single up the middle, Weaver went to his reliable bullpen. Tippy Martinez walked Reggie Jackson, and Weaver rose again from the dugout. Stoddard retired pinch-hitter Bob Watson on an infield bouncer, and the 4-2 lead headed to the ninth. Singleton had driven in an insurance run in the ninth as Murray laced his fourth hit of the contest. In notching save No. 17, Stoddard allowed just a Rick Cerone double.

The pennant chase of 1980 was alive at least for one day. Even the Yankees' outgoing slugger Jackson had to agree. After a 0-for-3 night, he stood one long ball away from the 400-homer mark.

"It's not a pennant race until the lead is down to four games," Jackson told the *Sun*.

However, Weaver wasn't taking anything for granted.

"It's one game," Weaver told the *Times*. "As far as anything in the future, it doesn't mean anything because we're going to have to go out and do it tomorrow. If we don't, this one's wiped out."

The O's skipper could have been more optimistic. Stone was the scheduled starter in game two of the series. And his defending AL champs were playing their best baseball of the season. The winning streak had stretched to seven games. The Yankees' lead was 7.5 games on the first day of August. Palmer's victory shaved that mark to a more manageable 4.5.

Six-game winner Luis Tiant was on tap to pitch versus Stone on August 9. But the 39-year-old master of moves had come up lame. Five days after a solid 8-inning effort versus Milwaukee, Tiant complained of a muscle strain in his lower left back. Exit the four-time 20-game winner and enter nine-game winner Tommy Underwood. It was on the last day of April when these same two hurlers went at it in Baltimore. Underwood did not survive a six-run deluge in the second inning and fell to Stone 7-4. It was Stone's second win of the season and his team's first over the Yanks in four tries.

A crowd of 48,109 had barely settled in when Bumbry took the left-hander's pitch to center for the game's first hit. He promptly swiped second base and then watched as the next three hitters did nothing. The Yankees did not pass on their first opportunity against the O's 17-game winner. Murcer pulled a one-out single to right. Three seasons before, Oscar Gamble and Stone had been teammates on the White Sox. This time, Gamble was Stone's adversary, and he turned on a pitch for a two-run homer. Gamble's sixth homer of the season traveled a good 425 feet and put the home team up a quick pair of runs..

The Orioles' offense would not panic two runs down. Ayala opened the second with a clean hit, but, like Bumbry in the opening frame, he too died at second. Dempsey opened the third with an opposite field two-bagger. Bumbry's second at-bat versus Underwood also went the other way. It hit the foul pole and in process knotted the game up a 2-2. It was just the speedster's fifth homer of the campaign.

"I thought at first, it might go foul," Bumbry told the *Sun*. "I was screaming, 'Stay fair, stay fair."

Singleton banged a double to right but Underwood escaped further trouble by fanning Murray and inducing Ayala to pop to left.

Stone didn't take to his new found prosperity especially well. Willie Randolph and Murcer chased each other around the bases after lacing singles. It was for Randolph his lone hit in 11 trips to the plate against Stone in 1980. The home team had runners on the corners with the heart of the batting order stepping up. And up came Gamble. He popped another one up, but this time it stayed in the park. Belanger collared it for out No. 1. Jackson was up next, and Stone issued a free pass. Homer No. 400 would have to wait.

"Four hundred has nothing to do with it," Stone told the *Times*. "Four hundredth or 800th, it's not on my mind. He's just not going to beat me in this game. If he's going to hit the ball out, he's going to have to hit it to left-center."

Jackson countered with a thought or two.

"I can hit a fastball out there," Jackson said in the *Times*. "But I can't take the flop curve and hit it 450 feet to the opposite field."

The Stone of 1980 had a plan in mind before battling the Yankees slugger.

"I didn't let Reggie Jackson beat me," Stone told this writer. "That year, I walked guys that hit me hard. I usually walked left-handers I couldn't get out. And that's how a walk became my best friend."

Stone indeed had learned his lessons against this future Hall-of-Famer. Entering this campaign, Jackson had chewed up Stone a Ruthian .714 batting average (5-7). Jackson would get a career-high 11 plate appearances against the right-hander in 1980. He would get a free pass in six of those trips.

Two-time Gold Glove first baseman Jim Spencer strolled to the plate with the sacks loaded and one out. He put one in the air but not out of the infield. DeCinces corralled it for a big second out. At 31-years-old, third baseman Eric Soderholm was in his final season in a Big League uniform. He, too, was Stone's teammate on that 1977 White Sox club. That was also the campaign in which he managed a career-high 25 round-trippers.

The string had played out. In a 2-2 tie, Stone faced a 3-2 pitch to his former teammate. Soderholm struck out swinging.

"Steve showed a lot of poise out there," said O's pitching coach Ray Miller to the *Sun*. "Especially after the first inning. And he really showed people something in that third inning."

By the middle frames, the Yankees' lefty seemed more in a groove. Underwood ran through the Birds lineup and retired 11 in a row heading to the seventh. Stone was not as sharp. Center fielder Ruppert Jones walked in the fourth and swiped a bag. In the sixth, he singled his way on and stole another base against the tandem of Stone and catcher Dempsey. Roenicke opened the seventh with a clean hit, but the O's offense went stagnant after that. In the Yanks half of the inning, Gamble laced a double past Singleton in right. Stone calmly intentionally walked Jackson and retired the side.

"This was not the gutsiest game of my career," Stone told the *Post*. "I was once hit in both legs when I was at Kent State and I finished the game."

The O's brought out their extra base hits in the eighth. Dauer's was of the two-bag variety. Singleton challenged Jackson's suspect glove in right and was rewarded a stand-up triple and RBI when the slugger just missed the drive.

"There is a little ledge at the top of the fence," Jackson told the *Times*. "The ball ticked my glove but didn't stick and it hit off that ledge."

Singleton's hot bat was another reason the O's were snapping back in the pennant race. Beginning of June 12, the switch-hitter had been hitting at a .366 clip with 31 RBI.

"He (Underwood) just got a fastball up," Singleton told the *Sun*. "And I really got into it. I've just been swinging the ball well off of everybody."

Underwood had given the Yanks seven strong innings. He gave way to Gossage and the Cy Young Award candidate stopped Murray on an infield bounce-out. He didn't have similar success with pinch-hitter Crowley, whose base knock up the middle plated a valuable insurance tally. It was 4-2 Baltimore.

"Gossage throws hard and you just have to prepare yourself and be ready," Crowley told the *Sun*. "I knew I hit the ball hard but I just wanted to see it land in center field. Now, I feel we've done our job here."

In the eighth, Jones made a dash for his third stolen base of the game. It failed and his two-out decision was not warmly received.

"I think Ruppert was trying to create something that wasn't there," said Yankees skipper Dick Howser. "He ran on his own. I think it's a case of trying to make things happen because we're struggling and not scoring runs."

Of course, Howser told a different story to the visiting writers from Baltimore.

"A guy who's been playing that long should know better," he said to the *Sun*. "That run didn't mean anything and it's not a good play."

Catcher Dempsey echoed Howser's second opinion.

"It was a stupid play," Dempsey told the *Sun*.

Even Weaver got into the middle of the rally-ending saga.

"What in the world did Rup say." Weaver asked the *Sun*. "He couldn't have been thinking."

It was more than enough to send the O's right-hander into the 18 win column. In the ninth, no Yankees player hit the ball into the outfield. The O's had knocked another game off the Yankees advantage. Stone was now 18-4 after the 4-2 win. In his last 17 decisions, the right-hander was 16-1. And afterwards, he admitted he left his famed curve ball back in Baltimore.

"I had to go with my slider," Stone told the *Sun*. "I don't think the Yankees have seen me throw one of those and I don't think my own club has much either. I used it extensively. You can't afford too many mistakes when you spot the other club two runs in the first inning. And I knew Underwood was going to pitch a good game."

The league's leading winner could now comment on the emerging pennant chase gripping the AL East.

"The thing we had to eliminate was an eight-game sweep by the Yankees," Stone said. "We've done that. I think the Yankees have taken us seriously all year. You always take the defending champions seriously."

The former Oriole Jackson was indeed taking the hot Orioles most seriously.

"They're playing hot right now," Jackson told the *Times*. "If they play like this all the way through, they're going to beat us. But if we hang on like men, we'll be OK."

The men from Baltimore had just won their eighth straight contest. Stone's loss in Texas was the only negative mark dating back 13 games. On July 25, the Birds stood nine games out and trailed not only the Bombers, but also the Tigers and Brewers. The winning spree had shaved away nearly six games off the margin. Stone's 18th win would pull the Birds within three games in the loss column.

With 32,000 fewer fans in the Oakland Coliseum, Norris took a no-hitter against Seattle into the sixth inning. That's when weak-hitting eighth-place hitting Mario Mendoza ended the suspense with a clean hit to left. The right-hander still took a one-hit shutout to the ninth. Norris completed his 3-hitter to go 15-7 on the season.

Another 15-game winner was on the mound on Sunday after-noon. Tommy John needed to get back into the Cy Young Award hunt and, most important, slow down the hard-charging Orioles. Flanagan would get the assignment as Baltimore looked to sweep the Yankees. The crowd of 54,123 wouldn't wait too long for the teams' offenses to kick in. After safeties by catcher Dempsey (hitting sec-ond) and Singleton, the Birds had runners on second and third with two down against John.

The Yanks loaded the sacks on a single, a DeCinces error and a walk. Both veteran pitchers escaped trouble, however, and this cru-cial contest sailed to the third scoreless. That's when the light-hitting Dempsey struck again. His seventh homer of the campaign put the Orioles up 1-0. Weaver had again completed his homework. Dempsey was a lifetime .300 hitter off of John. The O's weren't fin-ished. Murray would stroke the first of his three hits off of John to left field. Roenicke then cracked a run-scoring double and the Birds were up a pair. Second-sacker Lenn Sakata, batting .185 at the time, earned a rare start at second and made Weaver look good by chasing Roenicke home with the third run.

Flanagan evidently enjoyed the fireworks because he struck out both Jackson and Watson in the bottom half of the frame. Murray's opposite field two-bagger opened the visitor's fifth inning. Again Ro-enicke followed with a hit and Baltimore was up 4-0. And then the Yankees bats ignited. It was all tied at 4-4 when Sammy Stewart re-lieved in the sixth. Five hits, another DeCinces error and a sacrifice fly had erased the O's lead. The home team went for more in the sev-enth. Singles by Cerone and Jones put the Yanks up a run. It headed to the ninth. John was poised for another victory until Sakata drove one to deep left. Defensive replacement Bobby Brown seemed to get back in time but never touched the baseball. It fell for one of Sakata's four career triples. The tying run was 90 feet away with no one out. Getting a surprise hitting performance from the light-hitting Sakata, Weaver didn't push his luck. Shortstop Belanger was called back and the veteran slugger Lee May was called to battle against the lefty John. The 37-year-old former RBI champ made contact but his ball went directly in the glove of shortstop Dent.

The team's leading hitter (Bumbry) was scheduled to bat next. But again Weaver studied his scorebook. In four previous trips to the plate versus John, Bumbry failed to get the ball out of the infield. Weaver brought in the right-handed bat of Dauer. This reliable batsman made contact, lifting the baseball into left-center. That play was no problem for center fielder Jones. Sakata stayed at third but now there were two outs on the board and the Birds were still short a run. Dempsey was the Birds last hope. And this time Weaver stayed put.

"Do you know how many times I've pinch-hit for Dempsey in the ninth inning and watched the helmets go flying by?" Weaver said to the *New York Times*.

The count on Dempsey went to 2-2, and John fired a sinking fastball at the former Yankees backstop. This time, Dempsey delivered. His soft two-out clutch hit to center tied the game and stunned the home crowd.

"Tommy gets two outs with a man at third," Howser explained to the *Times*. "And Dempsey hits a ball off the ground into center field."

A flustered John walked Singleton and had to face Murray with the go-ahead run at second. Murray made him pay with a shot to right field that smacked off Jackson's chest for a run-scoring two-bagger.

The magic was back. The O's had taken a 6-5 lead in the ninth.

"It's just the way we've been getting beat," Dent was quoted by the *Times*. "We're making too many mistakes. We're beating ourselves. You just can't keep doing that day in and day out."

Stoddard mowed down the bottom of the Yanks' order for his second victory of the campaign.

Dempsey's last-second heroics had given the Orioles a three-game sweep of the division leaders.

"It was awfully high feeling," Dempsey told the *Times*. "I don't often get those opportunities. It might have taken a little bit of spunkiness out of the Yankees and that's what we have to do. Keep them down."

The three-game sweep of the home team certainly disappointed the Yankees' faithful. The fans themselves came through in droves. Exactly 156,362 crossed the turnstiles. A race that a Yankees' sweep would have effectively ended was now up for grabs. Just two games in the loss column separated the clubs and the pursuer was now riding a nine-game win streak. Now only if the schedule-maker had been a little kinder. For wedged in between the eight-game marathon with New York were three road games with the league's best team. The Birds were still unbeaten in the month of August as they boarded a plane to the Midwest. But 70-game winner Kansas City was not resting easy in the AL West. Despite a 13-game bulge over Norris and the Athletics, George Brett's team had won eight of 10 August contests and were quite content to sit at home and await the blistering hot club from Baltimore. The Yankees would lick their wounds but also leave the flying to the Orioles. While Baltimore's assignment was to fly halfway across the country to face a team 28 games above .500, the Yanks would stay at home for three games with the fifth-place Chicago White Sox (47-63).

The Yankees' lead stayed steady at 2.5 games after breaking their losing streak against the White Sox. There would be more late-inning dramatics in the Bronx on Tuesday the 12th. Ruppert Jones was the hero as his 10th inning grand slam gave the Yanks another sudden death victory, 8-4.

Death by base on balls is how the Orioles' 10-game winning streak concluded. 13-game winner McGregor did not enjoy Dennis Martinez's success against the Royals' big bats. Wilson and Brett each went 2-for-4. But a Brett miscue at third and a two-run hit from Singleton gave the Orioles three runs in the third. It was 3-3 before reliever Stoddard walked in the winning run.

Jim Palmer's Hall of Fame career is highlighted by 268 career victories, 2,212 strikeouts and a splendid career ERA of 2.86. What may not be as widely known is that in 3,948 innings of Major League baseball action the right-hander never allowed a grand slam. Of course he did give up some three-run homers. On Wednesday in Kansas City, Palmer was greeted by Wilson's 12th triple of the season. Wilson was already in the dugout with the game's first run when Willie May Aikens' 13th round-tripper of the season produced three more Royals runs. The 35,600 in attendance were barely into their first hot dog and Baltimore was already down four runs. Kiko Garcia's third inning two-bagger brought one run home to narrow the lead. But 10-game winner Rich Gale had his way with the Orioles' batting attack. Dan Graham and Rich Dauer were the lone hitters with more than one hit. Murray and Garcia had the only extra base hits (doubles). The Birds were handled 6-1 and were in serious danger of washing away the good deeds in New York. However there was some good news out of the Bronx, courtesy of White Sox right-hander Richard Dotson. He surrendered only a solo homer from the former Sox Oscar Gamble. His teammates supplied two sacrifice flies in the fifth inning alone and beat Ron Guidry and the Yanks 4-1. The winners were outhit 7-5.

The Sox had one single after the fourth inning. It didn't matter. Chicago salvaged a game of the series and spared the O's from losing further ground in the standings.

Thursday night was party night in Baltimore. The Yankees were coming. The Yankees were coming.

Just 48 fans short of the 50,000 mark poured into Memorial Stadium. For Baltimore, it was 18-game winner Stone. And nine-game winner Underwood would take the hill for the division leaders. Only five days separated the two Stone-Underwood matchups, but the visitors had made several changes in the batting order. Only second baseman Randolph, right fielder Jackson, catcher Cerone and shortstop Dent turned up in the same hitting positions. Center fielder Jones earned a promotion from the eighth spot in Howser's lineup to the second spot behind Randolph. Left fielder Gamble, who had doubled and homered off of Stone in New York, was now the designated hitter. The left-handed hitting Spencer sat down and was replaced by the right-handed swinging Watson. Judging by the book this was a good move. In Spencer's first 11 at-bats against Stone of old, Spencer had reached base six times. However, when Stone donned the Orange and Black of Baltimore, Spencer failed to reach first base his next dozen trips to the plate.

Eric Soderholm didn't earn rave reviews for his play in Stone's 18th win and was stationed on the bench, replaced by veteran Aurelio Rodriguez at third base. The Yankees left fielder on this night had just made his Major League debut in May. Joe Lefebvre batted 150 times this season and never would wear the Yankee pinstripes again.

The Orioles had made fewer changes in their attempt to beat Underwood again. DeCinces had managed a hit in four trips on Aug. 9. He sat down for the first game in Baltimore. Dauer batted second but moved from second base to third. Garcia earned a spot in the lineup with the vacancy at second. Dempsey, following his strong performance in New York, escaped the basement by moving up two slots in the batting order to the seventh spot. Stone's bid for win number 19 coincided with the 50th anniversary of the birth of Earl Sidney Weaver.

"I'd like to win all five," Weaver told the AP. "I know that's not probable because one of our pitchers is bound to make some kind of mistakes somewhere along the line. And we have to go against guys like Tommy John and Gaylord Perry and Guidry so I don't know. If we can win five, we could come out of the series a little bit ahead, and it's always better to be ahead. If we don't win all five, it means we'll have to win more games against the same competition afterward."

The nervous Yankees' front office had been busy planning for this critical five-game series. At 41-years-old, Gaylord Perry had already chalked up 285 of his 314 career victories heading to a date in Cooperstown. Texas handed the veteran to the Yanks in a late-season deal, and New York was clearly going to use him in this monstrous series.

In the opening frame of his 18th win in New York, Stone surrendered a long home run to former teammate Gamble. In his first trip to the plate in Memorial Stadium, Gamble again put the ball in the air. This time, he lost several feet by popping the ball behind the plate and into Dempsey's glove. That ended an uneventful first inning. Stone admitted afterwards that he abandoned his slider from his outing five days ago and went with the fastball that earned him notice in the All-Star Game.

"When you face the same team four days after beating them, you have to show them something different or you won't beat them again." he told the AP.

Bumbry had homered off of Underwood in New York. And the southpaw hurler, who would close his career four years later in an O's uniform, no doubt recalled the moment. Bumbry watched four pitches go by and strolled to first. Third baseman Dauer didn't wait around for a free pass. He stung one in the right-center gap and Bumbry used his legs to scoot home for the game's first run. The Birds weren't through. With first base open, Underwood gave Murray a base on balls. That strategy didn't pay off as Ayala spanked one up the middle and Dauer raced home from second giving the O's and Stone a 2-0 advantage.

In 1969, Hall-of-Famer Reggie Jackson bashed 47 homers for the Oakland A's. He retired in an A's uniform 18 seasons later with 563 career homers. Despite a career filled with memorable round-trippers, Jackson did not cross over the 40-homer plateau in any season but the 1980 campaign. He would hit an even .300 with 41 homers and a healthy 111 runs batted in. He didn't enjoy the same type of success against the O's pitching staff. In 41 trips to the dish, he would manage only six hits. Of course four of those safeties left the yard. And the O's two-run advantage was cut in half with Jackson led off the Yankees second inning with his 32nd homer of the season. With this shot, he opened a four-homer lead over Milwaukee's Ogilvie in the league race.

"I just have to keep on producing," Jackson told the *Post*. "If a ship is filled with holes in the hull, it still won't sink if the ship is strong enough. I just hope we don't have too many holes."

Stone wasn't set off course by the blast. He did issue a one-walk to Lefevbre but fanned Rodriguez to close the frame. Stone would have to face Jackson again in the third. And he was laboring somewhat. After two routine infield outs, both Jones and Gamble induced walks from the right-hander, bringing Jackson to the dish with two on and two down. Jackson's drive to center was hauled in by Bumbry, snuffing out the threat. The respective pitchers took it from there. Underwood had also learned a few things from his outing five days ago. Roenicke reached him for a single in the fourth but soon sat down when Dempsey rapped into a 5-4-3. twin killing. Dent slapped a clean hit to left in the fifth and stood on second with two out. That's as far as the 28-year-old shortstop would advance. After five full, the O's led the visitors 3-2 in the hit department. Hit No. 4 for Baltimore was a one-out single by Ayala. That was his second hit of the game.

Roenicke's second hit of the contest was minutes away. It was his sixth homer of the year and it was 4-1 Birds.

That was it for Underwood. His opposing hurler was finding a groove.

"Tonight, I gave them a lot of fastballs," Stone told the AP.

In the visitor's seventh, everything was center-cut. Bumbry took care of the drives of Cerone and Rodriguez. Dent bounced one to Garcia at second. The Yanks were stuck on two hits. With one out in the O's seventh something magical happened. Dauer caught up to a Ron Davis fastball and delivered it beyond the wall in left. It was 5-1 Birds, and more importantly, Dauer was off the hook.

"The hostage had been released. The pitchers have had him locked inside the park longer than the hostages in Iran," DeCinces joked to the *Post*.

All bad jokes aside, DeCinces had a point. Most astute baseball fans could point to the last time Dauer left the yard —Oct. 17, 1979 in Baltimore. The pitcher was Pittsburgh right-hander Jim Bibby,and Dauer's homer gave the Orioles a brief 1-0 lead in the seventh and deciding game of the 1979 World Series. The 27-year-old infielder had settled for singles and doubles in between. There were no three-baggers either. The slow-footed Dauer had three career triples in 3,829 plate appearances for Baltimore.

The homer gave Baltimore a bigger cushion and took the monkey off Dauer's back. However, there was no time for the Orioles to appreciate the moment.

Singleton was at the plate and he followed suit. Singleton's 15th homer seemingly put this game out of sight.

"When Singleton's ball was going out, I just watched Bucky Dent shrug at shortstop like he was saying, 'It's all slipping away.'" DeCinces told the *Post*. You could see it on their whole team tonight. The only one who's still carrying them is Reggie Jackson. They have great players and we respect them. But that game last Sunday had to break their backs. Now they're in our park, not theirs. And right at this moment, we are so hot and playing so well that we have the feeling there really isn't much they can do about it."

The deflated Yankees didn't get the ball out of the infield in the eighth. The two-hitter was intact. Stone came out for cheers in the ninth inning. After the game, he could reflect on what a difference a year made.

"It sure beats the Hell out of last year when 50,000 people were booing me when I was 6-7 and you had to give 10 of my baseball cards to get one of anyone else," he told the *Post*.

With a five-run advantage, Stone wasn't even bothered by the slugger Jackson leading off the frame. Jackson grounded out to Murray who took it to the bag. Watson drew a harmless free pass. The Yanks first baseman still went back to his hotel 0-3 on the night.

"He (Stone) doesn't give you a good ball to hit," Watson told the *Times*. "He throws at corners, spots his fastball and changes speeds. What happens is it looks so good to hit, guys are too anxious and they wind up swinging at his pitches."

Cerone was the final victim. He took a called third strike.

"We ain't hitting nobody right now," Cerone said. "They all seem difficult."

Yankees skipper Howser wasn't so precise as his team's lead in the East slipped to two games in the loss column.

"I'd like to give Stone credit," Howser said to the *Post*. "But I don't know if anyone is that good."

Despite walking five, Stone felt in control the entire contest.

"Tonight was typical," Stone said in the *Post*. "I took an inventory of my stuff and I made adjustments. My control was excellent as good as any time this year. My curve hasn't had as much bite after all the innings this year so I used my fastball more."

With the team's ace on a roll again, Singleton could see only good things happening the final six weeks.

"It was just a matter of time before we got everyone straightened out," he said. "I think we're there now, and the fans are coming back the way they were last year. The fans really have a way of turning us on, and getting a standing ovation before the game got started was good for us. It was very exciting and you could tell it was an important game. After all you don't get 49,000 out here every night."

With every victory of his magical campaign, Stone grew more and more philosophical.

"If I can't enjoy this year to the fullest, I ought to get out of this game as an ingrate," he said in the *Post*. "It's been a wonderful experience and I've relished every facet of it. You learn to savor the good when you're a .500 pitcher for so long. It's very exciting to pitch in a game like this. It's the kind of game where the fans are up and the players are, too. But there is a long way to go and tomorrow night we have to play the Yankees again. By then everyone will have forgotten about tonight."

Stone of 2005 did not forget much about the Yankees-Orioles series of 1980.

"The Yankees series was wonderfully exciting," Stone told this writer "The first time I beat them in that series, I threw all fastballs and curve balls. The second time, it was all fastballs and sliders. I went with two different plans. That Yankees team had some good left -handed hitters and I went 3-0. I had never beaten them before."

Pennant races were something new for Stone. As a rookie for the Giants in 1971, he was a member of a club that won the Western Division by single game. But Stone's contributions were minimal in the dog days. His last decision, a losing one, came on July 18. Flash forward to 1977. His 15-win season came as a member of the White Sox. That club won 90 games and also finished a dozen games off the pace. The Royals won 102 games. Texas (94-68) had a four-game advantage over Chicago for second place.

Stone's first team that won 100 or more games was the AL champion O's of 1979. But that team breezed to an eight-game lead over a quality Milwaukee club.

For the first time in his dull career, Stone was thrust into a battle for the top spot with the most famous baseball team in the world. On this night in Baltimore, Stone was the big league's biggest winner. He had just tossed a two-hitter at the first-place team. And his sense of humor was making it even more fun.

"In my other two-hitter, I lost 1-0," he said. "So I decided I wouldn't pitch any more of them."

Stone was now 19-4. He led the Major Leagues in victories.

At the Met, it took less than three hours to play a matinee involving the Twins and the visiting A's. Sensing victory, right-hander Norris struck out two of the final three Twins and pocketed a complete game for his 16th victory of the season.

In Baltimore, Stone's competition in the Cy Young race took the mound. John would battle Flanagan before another crowd of 50,000 at Memorial Stadium. And second baseman Randolph ended Flanagan's shutout bid on the first batter. It was the 25-year-old's sixth homer of the season. From one leadoff man to the other, Bumbry tied the contest with one swing of his bat. And it was also the Bee's sixth homer of the season. Bumbry wasn't fazed by the lefty-on-lefty matchup. And neither was the slugger Jackson. Flanagan had settled down in the early innings but faced Jackson with Lou Piniella on first in the visitor's fourth. His 33rd homer of the season made it 3-1. Ayala's second safety of the game came in the O's fourth but John again negotiated his way out of a slight jam.

By the fifth, the Birds were down three. Flanagan was gone and Stewart was working. And the O's kept on stranding runners. John was on a nine-inning pace to surrender a dozen hits. But runs are what count in this game. John surrendered his 10th hit of the contest to open up the seventh, and that was enough for Howser, who pulled John in favor of Doug Bird. After consecutive seasons with an ERA in the 5.00 range, Bird came to New York via the free agency route. And the change did him some good. His New York ERA was 2.66, and he went unbeaten in three decisions. But Dempsey reached Bird for a single following Bumbry's two-bagger. The Birds had something in the works. Singleton's sacrifice fly cut the lead in half. Gossage was called into a bases-loaded jam with just one out. Pinch-hitter Kelly caught one of the Goose's fastballs and ripped a shot towards right field. That's when defensive replacement Fred Stanley sprung into action, playing second base. His brilliant stop stopped the Birds from tying the contest. But first baseman Watson, nursing a sore finger, dropped the throw and it was a 4-3 game.

"The ball hit me right on my sore finger," Watson told the *Times*. "And I lost control of it. I was hurting all over after that."

The light-hitting Belanger (who *was* 7-for-17 lifetime versus Gossage) bounced to shortstop to end the threat.

"I just tried to throw it down the middle," Gossage told the *Times*. "I wasn't picking at spots."

Spots, eh? It's called the catcher's glove at about 100 miles per hour. In the eighth, the the AL's toughest player to fan stood in. Dauer struck out. And then Bumbry struck out. Singleton struck out to close the inning. Stone may have had the most wins in baseball, but no one was more dominating than the Goose. In the ninth, Murray and Crowley struck out. In 2⅓ innings of work in a one-run contest with serious pennant race implications, Gossage struck out five O's.

"Gossage was timed at 97 miles per hour," Weaver said in the *Times*. "Our gun is slow, so that means he was throwing 101 or 102. That's the highest we've ever timed here."

John picked up win No. 16. Gossage most certainly earned save No. 17. The Yankees had finally knocked off its top pursuer. The lead returned to 3.5 games.

"I keep looking in the paper, and we're still in first place," Cerone said. "And we're walking around here like a fourth-place team."

There was actually a better pennant race developing in the NL West. Houston, Los Angeles and Cincinnati each had 62 victories.

Gaylord Perry, a late-season pickup by the Yankees took the mound Saturday night in Baltimore. It was the 30th of July when the

Orioles last witnessed the offerings of Perry, then with Texas. On this night, Perry's mound opponent was the well-rested Dennis Martinez. 5.

The announced crowd of 51,649 had barely settled into their seats, when two batters into the contest, the visitors were up a run. Martinez scrambled out of further trouble by fanning both Jackson and first baseman Spencer. Murray led off the second with a 400-foot shot to center, but center fielder Jones kept it in the ballpark and turned it into the first out of the frame.

"That really gives you a lift," Perry told the *Times*. "It makes you proud to be with a team of championship quality."

It stayed 1-0 until the fifth, when Gamble's eighth homer of the season made it a 3-0 game. Crowley's two-out blast in the bottom of the inning cut the lead to two runs.

Soderholm matched that with his seventh homer of the season. Martinez actually pitched well in the 4-1 loss.

The Orioles' faithful had to feel badly about dropping 4.5 games out in this crucial series. But the fans did receive some free entertainment from their fiery manager. Weaver's famed temper got the best of him and he was naturally tossed. The visitors were certainly impressed.

"It was his best show yet," Perry said.

"I've never seen one like that," Gossage added.

In Kansas City, Gura just had to show up. The lefty went to 17-5 mostly because his Royals pounded the baseball. It was 8-0 entering the fifth. The Blue Jays reached him for five hits in the fifth but it was all over by then. Gura was very much alive in the Cy Young Award hunt with the 11-5 win.

Sunday was a critical afternoon for the Birds. Former Yankees farmhand Scott McGregor would try for his 14th win. His mound opponent, Tiant, had already logged 425 major league games before the O's southpaw threw his first pitch in the major leagues. Tiant was dazzling. McGregor was even better as 50,073 paid attendees were treated to a pitcher's duel. Crowley's two-out RBI double in the sixth chased home the only run of the contest. It took less than two and a half hours to play. The slugger Jackson fanned three times.

"The mystery is how I've been able to get my fastball by him," McGregor told the *Times*. "I've always had good success with it against him. I'm going to stay with it until he shows me he can hit it. I'm stubborn."

Jackson did manage one infield ground out to avoid a terrible afternoon.

"He pitched me opposite of how everybody else on the club pitched me so I was baffled," Jackson told the *Times*. "Every time up I took a pitch for a strike that I could have hit out of the park if I was looking for it."

Pivotal game five of this series would determine its winner. A Monday night in Baltimore didn't bother the gate receipts whatsoever, as 51.528 fans strolled through the Memorial Stadium turnstiles to see a classic matchup of Jim Pamer and Ron Guidry. Through three innings, the O's put runners in scoring position in two of the frames and failed to dent the plate. Palmer did not have such problems. He took a perfect game to the fourth. Murcer's one-out walk broke the streak at 10 in a row. The no-hitter and shutout vanished in one swing of Gamble's bat. His ninth homer of the season made it 2-0. The fourth was not kind to Guidry either. In fact, he didn't survive it. Three walks and two doubles later, it was 3-2 in favor of Baltimore. Rudy May put out any leftover fires and kept the Yanks in it. That is until he booted DeCinces' leadoff grounder in the fifth. Three runs later and Palmer was cruising at 6-2. He took that lead until the eighth when the Yanks erupted for three runs of their own.

This time, it was Tippy Martinez to the rescue, and it stayed at 6-5. Stoddard earned save No. 17 with two strikeouts in the ninth. The five-game series with the Yankees was over, as was the two–week stretch in which they faced each other eight times. And the Orioles had put themselves back in the ballgame with six wins. It was great for the game of baseball. Exactly 406,063 pushed through the turnstiles at both ballparks.

That's still well short of the figures set by the 2001 Montreal Expos (642, 745) but that number was notched in *81 games*. The five-game series in Baltimore drew 249, 605, which set a Major League record for a five-game series. The 156, 458 who sat in Yankee Stadium set an Orioles mark for a three-game road series, which still stands today. It was thrilling for fans and players alike.

"These were better-played games and a more intense rivalry than either the playoffs or World Series last season," Lowenstein told the *Sun*.

The veteran Belanger had played in four World Series. He found this series almost as thrilling.

"Great for the game," he said. "Great for the fans. But particularly great for us because we put them (wins) in the right column."

And of course, Weaver had to call for calm after taking the series 6-2.

"Everybody is too excited," Weaver said. "There will be times before this is all over when we think we have it all wrapped up. And there will be times when we may wonder what we have to do to win a game. This race will have so many ups and downs that people who haven't been around it before are going to get on and off our bandwagon four or five more times. But we won't. The guys in that room (locker room) will be on until we are three games down with two to go or until we've won it all."

August 23, 1980

American League East	W	L	Pct.	GB
New York	73	48	.603	—
Baltimore	72	48	.600	½
Milwaukee	67	57	.540	7½
Boston	63	55	.534	8½
Cleveland	63	57	.525	9½
Detroit	62	58	.517	10½
Toronto	50	70	.417	22½

Pitching Matchup

Baltimore (Steve Stone 20-4, 2.94) at Oakland (Brian Kingman 7-13, 3.34)

16

Pulling closer

After the biggest series of the season, the Cy Young chase shaped up with Stone leading in just one category-wins (19). John was three victories behind, but still led the AL in shutouts (six) and was third in innings pitched (196). Gura trailed Stone by just two wins and led the league in ERA (2.21), was second in shutouts (four) and fourth in games (14). Finally, Norris was tops in strikeouts (128) and second in ERA (2.32), innings (206) and complete games (18). The pennant race had not been decided by Aug. 18; nor had the chase for the coveted pitching award.

While Stone flirted with the no-hitter against the Majors' second-worst team, California, the Yankees and Underwood went further north Tuesday night to battle with the worst team in either league, the 42-76 Mariners. The Yanks doubled Seattle in hits (10-5), but it took some time to pin Rick Honeycutt with his 14th loss of the season, 3-1. Reggie Jackson's 34th homer of the season was good for the game's last run. The New York lead stayed at 2.5 games for another day.

The O's would take a modest four-game win streak into Thursday night's game in Anaheim. Angel-killer McGregor was in search of his 15th win. Dauer's two-run double erased an early Angels' lead. The ex-USC infielder went 4-for-4 in the Orioles 7-1 romp. And wouldn't you know, there some good news out of Seattle. The lowly Mariners had parlayed one Tom Paciorek single into four unearned runs, and Floyd Bannister had some runs to work with. But this was the Yankees after all, and by the fifth, New York had knotted the game up at 4-4. This time however, the Mariners didn't fold. Bruce Bochte singled in a run, and the Orioles were a game back in the loss column with 43 contests remaining.

In Oakland, the Orioles would miss a turn with Mike Norris. The 63-60 A's would not get so lucky with the 20-game winner Stone. Heading into his duel, Stone would know full well he was in the heart of a pennant chase. The Yankees and Orioles were now tied in the loss column. The Yankees' lead was down to ½ game.

Oakland right-hander Brian Kingman would also be a league leader in 1980. His 20 defeats paced the AL. Despite the dismal 8-20 mark, the 25-year-old right-hander pitched to a respectable 3.83 ERA and completed 10 of his 30 starts. In contrast, his mound opponent on this day finished nine of 37 starts. Of course, Oakland didn't have the luxury of a Stoddard and a Martinez to close out games.

Stone made some news in the first inning. He struck out both a young Rickey Henderson and Dwayne Murphy to open the festivities. By the second, the 20-game winner had some runs to work with. When the first two Birds reached base to open the second, Kingman looked in at the southpaw swinging catcher Graham. His eighth homer of the season to right-center put a three-spot on the board.

"Three-run homers will kill you especially with Steve Stone out there," Kingman told the *Oakland Tribune*.

The strikeout pitch was working again in the second. A single and a free pass gave Oakland some hope, but Tony Armas and Jim Essian went down on strikes to put Stone on pace for a complete–game, 18-

strikeout performance. Murphy was Stone's fifth fan job to close the third. When Henderson walked in the sixth, it broke Stone's streak of 11 batters in a row retired. He had followed up the no-hit bid in Anaheim with a 1-hit shutout through six full innings in Oakland.

That all changed in the seventh, when Mitchell Page came to the plate.

Page broke into the A's lineup in 1977. He hit a robust .307 but struck out 95 times. The next season his average dropped to .285, and he still struck out 95 times. His average plummeted to .247 in 1979, and he struck out 93 times. His four-year run as a successful hitter closed in 1980 when he launched 17 homers. The left-hander was right on Stone's pitches pulling both at-bats to the right side. He owned the home team's only hit entering the seventh. His next pull job went to the right field seats and his ninth homer of the campaign pulled Oakland within a pair of runs at 3-1. More trouble brewed from there. Catcher Jim Essian singled. Dave McKay was hit by a pitch 18 times during his 1,928 trips to plate. A full third of those chunks came in this year. Stone chipped one too close to McKay on an 0-2 count and the A's were in business as power hitter Wayne Gross came up to pinch-hit. Four years later, Gross would power 22 homers in an O's uniform.

Weaver took no chances. He opted for the lefty-on=lefty matchup with Tippy Martinez. Stone was done for the day, departing with a three-hitter and six strikeouts. However, the tying run was on first. He would again rely on his bullpen to protect the lead.

"This was a typical game for us," Stone said in the *Oakland Tribune.* "I need a few runs, a few good plays and a good job from the bullpen."

Unlike Baltimore, Oakland wasn't beaming hot air and humidity at the O's prized right-hander.

"I'm used to pitching in 95-degree weather and 95-percent humidity," Stone told the *Sun.* "Today I felt like I was throwing in a meat locker. And I told Earl after the sixth that I was feeling the effects. There is no sense being a hero at the club's expense."

Martinez wouldn't get his shot at the free-swinging Murphy. Instead, Billy Martin opted for the power bat of Jeff Newman (15 homers). Martinez struck him out. But Tippy wasn't his usual sharp self. He walked Jim Heath, the third pinch-hitter of the frame. The A's crept closer when Martinez uncorked a wild pitch past catcher Graham, scoring Essian. With Stoddard loosening in the pen, Martinez looked in at Rickey Henderson and was given the sign not to pitch to him. He was given a free ticket to first.

Martinez recalled this exact game 23 years later and picked up the play by play.

"I went 3-2 on the next hitter (Murphy)," Martinez said. "I could not throw another strike. I just knew it. Murphy just can't hit me at all. He knew that and I knew that. It was a matter of throwing the ball over the plate. Steve was still going crazy. Eddie got a whiff of it. You kind of feel things. So we put on a pickoff move. So I did the pickoff move and picked Henderson off first base. And that was the end of the inning."

Yes, Henderson, the Hall of Famer known for his baserunning prowess, was caught napping at first with the bases filled with A's. It possibly cost Oakland the ball game. He blamed his first base coach, Lee Walls.

"The first base coach told me to get off, get off," Henderson told the *Tribune*. "To me, it's his fault. I can' t see the guy coming from behind me. But then again, I didn't have anywhere to go with the winning run on second so I was pissed off at myself but I don't think it was my mistake. If I had done what I was going to do, I would have been on top of the bag."

Henderson was born Christmas Day, 1958 in Chicago. That baseball season in Chicago was highlighted by Walls' selection to the National League All-Star team. The veteran of 10 major league seasons wasn't going to take anything from a young player, even if he was the stolen base king in 1980.

"It's a high school play," Walls told the *Tribune*. "Where are you going with the winning run on second?"

Weaver in the O's dugout took credit for the play that helped decide this contest.

"The little diamond," Weaver told the *Sun*. "That's the play we always work on down on the little diamond in spring training. And today it paid off. It's the play I lose my voice on every spring. Give credit to Eddie. He put it on. All I can do is teach it to them. They have to execute it."

The A's volatile manager Billy Martin was almost gracious in losing on the pick-off play.

"It's a great play," Martin told the *Post*. "But it should never happen. What could be more embarrassing? We didn't just crawl out from under a rock. We know that play exists."

Stone's 21st victory was back on track after the stunning turn of events at first base.

"That pick-off play is one of the great plays I've seen in the last two years," Stone said. The 20-game winner in the dugout noted Martinez's daring play.

"I got out of the inning and he was so happy," Martinez said. "He was right next to me when I got out of the inning. He said, 'One more inning.' He was always pulling for you."

Martinez returned to erase Murphy opening the eighth. But a two-base error charged to Bumbry put the tying run in scoring position again. Enter Big Foot. And this night Stoddard was humming the ball. Tony Armas and Mitchell Page whiffed at his offerings.

"After facing Stone and all those breaking balls, it looks like Stoddard is up there throwing 150 miles per hour," Page told the *Tribune*.

Graham's second homer of the contest opened the ninth. And Stoddard fanned the side in the bottom of the ninth. Stone was now a 21-game winner, and the O's had held serve.

"Tim Stoddard came in and shut the door," Stone said in the *Tribune*. "That's the ninth game he's saved for me this year."

"I felt good out there," Stoddard told the *Sun*. "I guess I did have a little extra, but it feels good to have it because that means you don't have to set up hitters with your slider. Today, I was able to throw high strikes because my ball was moving enough."

Weaver wasn't going to claim Stoddard was the equal of the Yankees' Goose Gossage.

"No, he's better than Gossage," Stone told the *Post*. "He beats himself less. People forget Stanley (Don Stanhouse) lost his job to Tim last year. He only got it back because Stoddard got hurt."

The 21 victories was tops in the majors. Like 19-game winner Steve Carlton of the Phillies, Stone owned a four-victory advantage over his nearest competitors. Lefty held his lead over 15-game winners Jim Bibby of the Pittsburgh Pirates and the Dodgers' Jerry Reuss. Stone's three Cy Young competitors stood at 17 wins. On May 5, the right-hander lost 4-2 to the Twins. Since that time, he had wheeled off a 19-1 record. And his team had finally caught up with him. Both Stone and the Orioles were playing their best baseball of the season.

"We are just blowing people out," Stone told the *Post*. "It's typified by that big guy right there (Stoddard)."

The young catcher Graham was the hitting hero of win No. 21.

"Two days after the All-Star break, Ray Miller came to me and said, 'You wait and see. This team will catch fire, and you're going to have more fun playing baseball than you ever dreamed possible. You will not believe the way this team plays.'

"It's true. Look around. Very few guys are totally outstanding. We might have three all-around stars and that's being generous. But jeez, look what we do together."

The victory was the Orioles' seventh in a row. The August mark was an improbable 18-4. Since Stone's masterpiece in the All-Star game, Baltimore's record was 31-12. From the middle of June to Aug. 23, the Birds had played at a Ruthian clip of .714 (45-18).

"We've played about .800 baseball for weeks," Belanger told the *Post*. "You've just got to milk that and ride it for all it's worth. Everybody is healthy. Everybody is hot."

The pennant chase would continue on when the respective clubs took the field on Sunday, the 24th. Flanagan took advantage of three double play grounders and won his ninth straight game over Oakland, 3-0.

"It seems like these trips are always our best," Flanagan told the AP. "Maybe it's because we have a lot of West Coast guys on the team, and they like to show off out here"

Former Yankee star Martin weighed in on the pennant chase in the AL East.

"I'm rooting for the Yankees because my friend is Dick Howser." Martin told the AP "I wish we'd beat Baltimore three straight."

If it had rained hard after 5 innings in Anaheim, the O's would have slipped into first place, maybe for good. Former O's second baseman Grich had ripped a two-run single, and the Yanks were down 2-1 heading to the sixth. Martin's loyal friend, Howser, pulled Guidry. Gossage cleaned up, and Grich fanned to end the game. The ½-game lead stood for another day in the 5-2 Yankees win.

The heat was still on though. Baltimore's latest winning streak stood at eight games.

"This is the kind of baseball we're playing every day now," Weaver said. "Getting good pitching and winning with one swing of the bat."

Seemingly, the advantage swung to Baltimore. New York would be next to visit Oakland but would run immediately into 17-game winner Norris. The O's would hop up the Pacific Coast and to meet the Majors' worst team in Seattle. Actually, three American League hurlers chased their 18th win on Monday night. In Milwaukee, Gura opposed 14-game winner Moose Haas. The key matchup, of course, was Norris and John in Oakland. Stone and his comrades would root for Norris and let Dennis Martinez pitch them into first against the weak Mariners.

However, this was Major League Baseball, and nothing goes as planned. A Bumbry double, a balk by well-traveled Glenn Abbott, and a Dauer safety put the Birds up a run. Before fewer than 7,000 in the Kingdome, the Mariners showed Martinez an early exit. A six-spot went up on the board in the opening frame and the visitors were stunned.

Murray's 22nd homer in the fourth pulled Baltimore within a grand slam. Singleton's two-run shot in the eighth produced some help, but Murray was caught trying to turn a double into a triple and the eight-game win streak was history, 10-5.

There was clearly more interest in Oakland that night. More than 49,000 pushed the turnstiles to see Billy Martin's gang mess with their boss' former employer. The fiery Martin had guided the Yanks to two American League Championships and one World Series crown during his intermittent five-year stay in the Bronx. He also was the manager for the first part of 1978 before George Steinbrenner axed him in favor of Bob Lemon. Lemon led the Yankees to a stunning comeback in the divisional pennant race and a World Series title, but was whacked in 1979 with Martin taking over. After a tumultuous half-season in New York in 1979, Martin found himself as manager of the A's.

John was the first to blink under the Oakland spotlights. It was 5-0 Norris and the A's after two. John did make it to the fifth before passing off to Gaylord Perry. Norris passed them both on his way to his 19th complete game and 18th victory of the season, 9-1.

Three times during the 12-year voyage of Bruce Anton Bochte, the California native scored exactly 58 runs in a season. In 1980, he fell just one run short of tying that mark again. He scored in the ninth inning of Tuesday night's game in the Kingdome. It was his 10th homer of the season and it ended a pitching duel between the Mariners' Floyd Bannister and the O's McGregor. Bochte drove in both Seattle runs in the heartbreaking 2-1 loss. It might have been the O's best chance at finally moving into the top spot in the AL East. That's because in Oakland, Martin's club was again giving the Yankees fits. Rick Langford went the distance for his 14th win. It was his 19th straight complete game. That left the right-hander one game short of Robin Roberts' Major League record, set in 1953. The A's prevailed 3-1.

"I just went power to them in the ninth inning," Langford said in the next day's *New York Times*. "I didn't want to walk anybody. Sometimes that can get a rally started and wind up hurting you more than a home run."

Naturally, Martin went on the defensive after his team took two straight from New York.

"People say I held back Mike and Rick for the Yankees," Martin told the *Times*. "That is certainly not true. It's the way the rotation came up. I have to listen to people say we couldn't beat the Orioles. Don't they know I would love to beat the pants off Earl Weaver? So what happens-they go to Seattle and lose two."

Still trailing by a scant ½ game, the O's took Wednesday off and headed home to face the Angels. The Yankees also said goodbye to the West Coast and would return to the Bronx and try and cool down those suddenly hot Mariners. The O's bats had mysteriously cooled in Seattle. The flight home did that wood some good.

Roenicke, Murray and Dauer each recorded a four-hit night Thursday against California. Roenicke would double in three of those at-bats. Crowley and Bumbry would notch three hits each. Officially, it was 18 singles and eight two-baggers. The 26 safeties in a nine-inning game remains an Orioles record. The eight doubles tied a club mark. It was 11-2 by the fourth inning and Palmer would breeze from there.

In winning his 14th game, Palmer surrendered 11 hits but claimed a 13-8 decision. The two clubs combined for 40 hits. In New York, the Mariners put up a 3-spot in the sixth to knot the game up at 5-5. Murcer's seventh-inning leadoff homer decided this game. The Yanks held on again 6-5. This night also marked the final day of the ½ game lead. Baltimore would never again be this close to first place.

August 29, 1980

American League East	W	L	Pct.	GB
New York	76	50	.603	—
Baltimore	75	50	.600	½
Boston	67	56	.545	7½
Detroit	66	59	.528	9½
Cleveland	65	50	.520	10½
Milwaukee	67	63	.515	11
Toronto	52	74	.413	24

Pitching Matchup

California (Fred Martinez 3-6, 4.97) at Baltimore (Steve Stone 21-4, 2.94)

17

Never again

On paper, it was no contest. On Friday night, 21-game winner Stone would oppose three-game winner Fred Martinez. The 23-year-old right-hander from Los Angeles would make 23 starts for the 1980 Angels. He would never start another game. His previous start came against the Yanks and he went six full innings, allowing just five hits.

More than 33,000 were in the stands on Aug. 29 expecting to see Stone knock off the rookie. Plus, the O's seemingly had the Angels' number. The previous night's victory was the 11th straight over the Halos. Stone went after an even dozen victories and fanned Rick Miller to open the festivities. But a Carew single and a Baylor two-bagger produced a two-out run for California. In his six years in an O's uniform, Baylor ripped out 76 doubles. This run-scoring tally was a routine fly ball that somehow fell between shortstop Garcia and left fielder Lowenstein. There would be more trouble in the second. But Stone negotiated a first and third situation. Instead of fanning Miller, he induced the southpaw-swinger to bounce into a rally-killing double play.

Just 24 hours after a hit parade at Memorial Stadium, the O's bats were silenced, unable to solve the less than stellar offerings of Martinez.

"A lot of our guys kept saying he didn't have anything," pitching coach Ray Miller told the *Sun*. "But he kept on getting everyone out."

Rick Miller would get the last laugh. With two runners on in the fourth, he clocked a triple clearing the bases. The Cy Young candidate was down 4-0.

"For the first five innings he threw 88 and 89 miles per hour, while Steve was struggling with his control." Ray Miller said.

In the fifth, another ex-Oriole struck back. Grich banged a shot up the middle that Stone made a stab at. In his haste to make a play, Stone fired a ball into the dirt at first, and Jason Thompson touched the plate for the Angels' fifth run. Adding insult to his injury, Stone departed after the Grich liner. In less than five innings of work, Stone was touched for seven Angels hits and four earned runs. His four walks didn't help the cause either. It was his shortest outing since that black day in Texas on the final day of July. Stone had not dropped a decision in Baltimore since early May. However, it was not ground in stone that a loss would go on Stone's record. Reliever Ford put together one of his best outings of the season. He allowed just two hits the rest of the way and no runs. In the sixth, Bumbry reached third but Singleton couldn't drive him home. In the bottom of the ninth, the Birds laced three singles. A double play put brakes on the rally, and Crowley's bounce out to first sealed Stone's fifth loss of the season, 5-0. Martinez would go the distance and scatter six singles.

"I'm kind of getting tired of people telling me I don't belong here," Martinez said. "I don't agree. We were going bad and people wanted to pin the blame on somebody. I don't think it was fair to pin it on me."

Martinez also found a way to beat Stone at Memorial Stadium. Dating back to June of the previous season, Stone had won 16 of 17 decisions at the park on 33rd Street.

To make matters worse, another Cy Young candidate picked up some ground this night. Heading to the home half of the seventh in the Bronx, John and Seattle's Rob Dressler were locked in a 1-1 tie. Watson's 2-run homer in the home half was the telling blow in the Yankees' 5-1 win. John picked up win No. 18 and worse for the Orioles, the New York lead was now 1.5 games.

The Yanks' lead would continue to creep upwards. After watching the team ace lose to California on Friday, Flanagan didn't survive the first against the suddenly potent Angels.

Carew's triple led off the frame and four runs later, Tippy Martinez was called upon for rare first-inning help. Murray's three-run homer off Frank Tanana brought 38.000 to their feet, but Carew's second two-bagger of the game made it 6-4 Halos in the fourth. Jason Thompson's pinch-hit 3-run homer off of Stoddard clinched it in the eighth. California banged out 15 hits in the 12-6 win.

In New York, Larry Milbourne's fifth inning single tied the game at 2-2 heading to the home half of the inning. Brian Doyle and Murcer both batted twice in the Yankees turn. It was a six-run frame and Gaylord Perry, and New York took it from there, 9-3. bringing the lead now to 2.5 games. The O's had dropped four of five.

Actually, the A's visit to Fenway outdrew the O's game by close to 10,000. Were the Bosox fans all that interested in spotting Cy Young Award candidate Norris? Boston had pulled within five games of the Orioles for second. The A's stood an even 20 games back of the high-flying Royals. Norris would be opposed by a lefty who would be in a Cy Young chase in five years. John Tudor was still short of 20 major league starts in a distinguished career that would conclude with 263 such performances.

Norris came out firing. Perez, Fisk, and designated hitter Dave Rader all went down on strikes in the second. Norris would settle for

11 strikeouts in less than 7 innings of work. Tudor's work was cleaner and the A's right-hander slipped to 18-8 in the 5-1 loss at Fenway.

More than 43,000 poured into Yankee Stadium to see the division leader put Seattle out of its misery. But the lefty Bannister pitched shutout ball into the sixth before his back went out on him. Tiant was even more effective for New York firing a shutout at the Mariners for eight full frames. A rare Randolph fielding error chased home the lone run of the game in the ninth and made a loser of reliever Guidry. The 1-0 shocker in the Bronx sliced the lead to 1.5 games.

On the final day of August, Stone's 21 wins was still ahead of his nearest competitors by three victories. Norris, Gura and John each stood at 18. Norris paced the junior league in strikeouts (149) and was second in complete games (19), innings (230⅓) and ERA (2.34). John topped the circuit in shutouts (six), and Gura was top in ERA (2.28).

The O's and Weaver had a strong reputation for playing their best baseball in the last month of the season. Since the O's juggernaut lifted off in 1969, Weaver's clubs had posted just one losing record from the last day of August until the final bell. That mark was etched during the 1972 campaign. Weaver's teams managed 20 wins or more in seven Septembers prior the 1980 season.

On Labor Day, Dennis Martinez would get a second chance at the Mariners who belted him around the Kingdome six games earlier. A quick 2-run first inning settled him in with an early lead. Singleton's second homer of the contest and 20th of the season made it 4-1 in the fifth.

Seattle roughed up Stoddard in the ninth, and Tippy Martinez had to put out the fire with the tying run at second. The 77th win of the season was in the books, 5-4. In New York, the visiting A's lashed three doubles against the lefty Underwood – and just one more single.

The southpaw, who dropped three decisions to Stone prior to this outing, was never better. His four-hit shutout bested complete-game ace Rick Langford 5-0 in less than two hours.

Fewer than 8,000 showed to see Palmer beat the Mariners. On Wednesday night, (Sept. 3) that number jumped to 12,110 as Stone made a go at win No. 22. That same night, more than 27,000 were on hand in New York to see John hunt for his 19th victory. In the first round of the 1972 baseball amateur draft, the Giants selected 18-year -old Rob Dressler. Four years later, they watched the 6-foot-3 right-hander lose 10 of 13 decisions. San Francisco cut their losses. Four years later, he would drop 10 of 14 games while toiling for Seattle in 1980. Needless to say, he didn't make it out of spring training the fol-lowing season. Dressler and Stone would be the mound opponents on this night in Baltimore.

There was some action in the Mariners first. Joe Simpson went up the middle for the game's first safety. Bruce Bochte drew a two-out walk from Stone giving contact hitter Tom Paciorek two runners on with two out. Stone struck out the 33-year-old first baseman.

"Stone mixes up his pitches so well, it is almost impossible for a right-hander to hit him," Paciorek told the *Sun*. "His slider moves so well over the plate, and he just keeps you off-balance all the time."

Paciorek would repeat that strikeout in the Seattle fourth. By this time, Stone had found his groove as 13 consecutive Mariners went back to the dugout without reaching base. In all fairness, Dressler had pitched well against the 21-game winner as well. Veteran Shane Rawley provided Seattle with one-out relief in the sixth. A leadoff walk of catcher Larry Cox in the Mariners' half of the sixth ended the streak, but by this time, Stone and the Birds were up a pair of runs. The visitors' sixth would challenge Stone. After the free pass to Cox, leadoff man Julio Cruz punched one up the middle and Cox hustled off to third, putting runners on the corner for Simpson, Danny Meyer and Bochte.

Simpson was the first to fail. His pop up to the right side of the diamond didn't clear the infield. Dauer collared it for the big first out. Meyer was next up and did his best to tire out the O's ace. "While I was pitching to him, I hit all the spots that I wanted," Stone told the *Sun*. "I threw all four of my pitches in every zone, and he kept fouling them away. I got him with a good curveball. Low and a little off speed. That might have been my best duel of the season."

Meyer manage to sky the ball to right field, but Cox didn't test Singleton's strong right arm in right. Bochte's fly ball settled into Lowenstein's glove in left for the inning's third out.

Weaver couldn't have been much prouder of Stone after he averted serious problems in the frame.

"Right there, I would have given him two runs, just to get out of the inning." Weaver said. "I felt he was going to hold them the rest of the way, although he did eventually give up a run. In that situation, he went out and did a hell of a job concentrating on the hitters."

After the contest, Stone commented to the *Baltimore Sun* on the work behind the plate of umpire Dallas Parks.

"There was a discrepancy over my curves," Stone said. "I don't think he (Parks) has called one of my games and he had to get used to my style. I throw two types of curves. One that comes in high and breaks around the belt and one that starts at the belt and breaks at about the knee.

"So I asked him if he was going to give me the high one. If he would give me the other one. He said he would so I adjusted and he called a pretty consistent game after that."

Pitching coach Miller spotted what concerned Stone.

"I think the ball was breaking a little more than Dallas realized," Miller said. "There is a tendency for a young umpire to call the big breaking pitch out in front of the plate."

Seattle manager, Maury Wills wasn't concerned with Stone's curveball. He put his emphasis on how the heart of his batting order did nothing to help the disturb the man on the mound.

"Tonight, I had my three best guys up there (with runners) in scoring position but we came up empty," Wills told the hometown *Seattle Times*. "I'm not putting any pressure on them or distracting them with rules and demands. Stone is a good pitcher, but he was no Hall of Famer out there tonight. We had some pitches to hit."

It was 2-0 Orioles heading to the seventh. Dauer's single had plated one run in the previous inning, but center fielder Simpson beat Lowenstein with a throw to the plate to keep the third run away for the time being.

Paciorek managed contact for the first time in this contest when he opened the seventh with a weak pop to the left side. Stone had another 1-2-3 frame. In the visitor's eighth, Simpson again made some noise. The 6-foot-3 left-hander from Oklahoma managed only nine career homers in a shade under 1,400 trips to the plate, but on this night in Baltimore, he had exactly half of his team's safeties. With Cruz on first and two down, Simpson cracked his 11th two-bagger of the season and Cruz raced home to carve the O's lead to a slim 2-1.

The Birds took the suspense out of the contest in the home half. Murray, Roenicke, Dempsey and Garcia each earned RBI in the frame as Stone's 22nd victory was three outs away in a 5-1 contest. Paciorek's fourth trip to the dish produced his fourth out. There was some solace for him as he managed to hit the ball into the outfield for the first time all night. Larry Milbourne's bounce out to defensive replacement Sakata at short made it official.

Stone's four-hit complete game moved his season mark to a daunting 22-4.

"He's got a curveball as good as anyone's in the American League," Weaver told the Associated Press. "If he can throw it for strikes when they're not looking for it, they've got no chance.

"Stone just throws the pitches he wants you to hit," "He throws the ball over the plate and tells the batter to try and hit it. He gives them what they aren't expecting and gets them out."

Add this 22nd win to his career total and it made a clean century. In his 249th big league start, Stone had collared his 100th career victory.

"One hundred was a long time coming," Stone told the *Post*. "And I'm glad to get it. I ought to get to a hundred four or five before the season's over."

Stone walked just two in the complete game. But that increased his free pass total to 82. That moved him into a tie for fourth place in the league for most walks. Stone and the A's Steve McCatty were one walk behind Oakland's Matt Keough. There was no danger of catching the league leader, Toronto's Jim Clancy, whose 110 walks gave him a healthy lead.

Stone's ERA dropped to a cool 2.96, which was tops on the club for both starters and relievers. The 100th win meant a full third of his major league victories had come in not quite two seasons with the Orioles.

"I had never played on a team that good before," Stone told this writer. "I played on the Giants team with Mays, McCovey, Gaylord Perry and Bobby Bonds. That was a good team. But the 1979-80 Orioles were a great team. It was an excellent team. It's hard just to get ready to play 162 games. But the Orioles knew how to play winning baseball."

Meanwhile, the Yankees were in New York needing a win over Oakland to maintain their lead in the division race. In the Yankees' first, both Willie Randolph and Bucky Dent increased their triple totals by one as New York put a four-spot on the board. John was in very good shape heading to the second inning in the Bronx. Mitchell Page's 12th homer of the season in the second inning was just a solo shot, and Ricky Henderson's sac fly in the third cut the New York lead in half. New York answered with long balls from Oscar Gamble and Jim Spencer.

John fanned seven and surrendered five hits in hurling a complete game. He was very much in the Cy Young race at 19-7. Furthermore, the New York lead stayed still at 1.5 games. Like Stone, John used brain power to overpower American League hitters.

"The way I pitch," John once told *Sport* Magazine. "Is a lot like the way Gene Littler hits a golf ball. You can see his easy swing, and you say he can't hit it that far, but he's out there with them. You don't have to be a grunt to crank out a long drive.

"The art of pitching is making the hitter think you're throwing the ball harder than you are or slower than you are.

"There is a difference between throwing strikes and throwing strikes. The plate is 17 inches wide. You're throwing from the inside three inches to three inches off the plate. You are throwing to a foot but you take out the middle of the plate. A strike is not just to lay the ball over the plate but to throw the ball over the corner. That's the art of pitching. And that's what a lot of guys in baseball never acquire."

Another paltry crowd of 12,000 scattered through Memorial Stadium to see Flanagan welcome in Billy Martin and the A's. By the fifth inning, those fans could depart without guilt. Despite picking off two runners in that frame, Oakland and pitcher Matt Keough were up 6-0. Oakland ripped off 15 hits and took a small bite out of the Orioles chances with a 7-1 decision.

In the Big Apple, the division leaders hosted the California Angels. Randolph and Dent led off the Yankees' first this time with back -to-back singles. New York struck Angels lefty Frank Tanana for three first-inning runs. California pulled within 4-3 in the sixth on a Bobby Grich RBI. Usually a starter, Ron Guidry picked up his first save of the season with three strong innings of relief and New York's lead went up to 2.5 games with the 5-3 win.

Friday night's matchup in Baltimore brought together McGregor and Oakland's Norris. The A's pushed the O's southpaw up against the ropes in the very first frame. Armas would stroll to the plate with the sacks loaded and no one out. Luckily for McGregor and his teammates, the right fielder bounced to Murray but earned an RBI for this trouble. Norris would face Baltimore in home half with some rare run support, as McGregor surrendered three first inning runs. And with 24,000 looking on, the O's went 10 up and 10 down. Any dreams of a perfect game vanished in the fourth when third baseman Dave McKay booted a Dauer grounder. Singleton made the A's pay for their clumsiness with his 21st homer of the season to put the Birds in business.

The home run evidently rattled Norris. He walked Kelly, and then had him picked off first. However, in his haste to earn a quick out, Norris fired the baseball past first baseman Jeff Newman, and Kelly earned an extra base for his trouble. One inning later, the same scenario played out. This time, the baserunner was Garcia after a two-out single. Norris earned his second error in two innings when his missed Newman again as Garcia grabbed an extra bag. Norris entered the contest with one miscue in his previous 234 innings of work.

Armas led off the sixth with his 30th round-tripper of the season, and Norris was up a pair at 4-2. His lead grew steadily. Norris didn't answer the bell in the O's eighth, but it didn't seem to matter. Oakland had chased McGregor and Baltimore trailed 6-2. In the eighth, they settled for a three-run homer off the bat of Ayala.

Reliever Stoddard struck out the first two hitters of the ninth but didn't complete the trifecta. Oakland manufactured a two-out run and again things looked hopeless at 7-5.

The fifth Oakland error helped the home team's cause in the bottom of the ninth. That made all three O's runs unearned. Singleton, who led the Majors in game-winning hits at 19 doubled to right to steal a sure victory from Norris and the A's. In one of the more heroic victories of the season, the O's prevailed 8-7.

Meanwhile, the O's had a glimmer of hope coming from the Bronx. Rick Miller led off the California first with only his second round-tripper of the season. In the fourth, Larry Harlow used manager Weaver's favorite at-bat, the three-run homer, to help chase starter Tiant. The Angels had a 5-2 lead behind southpaw Ralph Botting. Of course, this was a pitcher who in 18 career games in an Angels uniform pitched to an unthinkable 7.39 ERA.

His seventh inning wild pitch led to trouble. And so did a Carney Lansford error and a Dave Skaggs passed ball. The Yanks tied it at 5-5 after seven.. It went 10 innings, but the Angels never had another runner reach base. Willie Randolph's single won it, 6-5. The Birds stayed pat at 2.5 games out.

Stone's bid for his 23rd win would come on Sunday afternoon. His 21st victory had come in Oakland, and this time on Sept. 7, he would face right-hander Steve McCatty in Baltimore.The A's, three games under the .500 mark, did have something to play for. In addition to the battle for second place with Texas, the 1980 A's would leap into the Major League record book if McCatty could complete the matinee job. The 1968 San Francisco Giants,

led by Juan Marichal's league leading 30 complete games, finished with 77 complete games in a 162-game schedule. McCatty's complete game would be No. 78. Ironically, the 1941 Chicago White Sox staff tallied 106 contests with no relief but did it during the 154 game schedule.

Stone began this contest as if he wouldn't even complete the first inning. He walked Rickey Henderson, who apparently recalling the egregious pickoff play in Oakland, successfully negotiated second base for his league-leading 72nd stolen base of the season. Dwayne Murphy then roped a hit to center, and Bumbry went home with the throw. Naturally, Henderson beat the tag at the plate, and Murphy scampered to second base. He didn't have to wait long. Dave Revering banged his 20th double of the season, and it was very quickly 2-0.

Oakland wasn't through with the 22-game winner. Wayne Gross also sent the ball up the middle to Bumbry, and Revering was soon in the dugout as his team was up by three runs.

McCatty didn't close the door just then. The first three hitters of the third inning reached base against the 26-year-old. An infield error and a Murray sacrifice fly pulled the O's and Stone within a single run at 3-2. The A's responded in kind. The first three hitters of the visitor's fourth also reached base. Aided by an O's error (Garcia) and a suicide squeeze, Oakland matched the two-run frame with one of its own and led 5-2. Stone did earn the satisfaction of making Henderson look at strike three.

From the sixth inning on, the Cy Young Award's leading candidate did not allow another Oakland hitter to reach base. He retired the final 12 batters in a row.

McCatty wasn't as sharp. Garcia doubled in the fourth. Crowley singled in the sixth. Murray singled and reached third base in the eighth. However, the rest of the O's offense did not come to the rescue in a 5-2 defeat. Stone's mark slipped to 22-6 despite his complete game eight-hitter. McCatty and his A's had their record. And for McCatty, who would pitch all of his nine Big League seasons in an Oakland uniform, it was just his eighth start-to-finish performance. He was still well behind Rick Langford (24) and Norris (19). Brian Kingman was in third place on the A's with nine. The record was hardly any concern to Baltimore, though. The Birds had lost three of four to Oakland.

"They play well against Western Division teams," said Oakland first baseman Dave Revering in the *Oakland Tribune*. "I don't think they've had it because they're pitching is so good. But if they drop another game, they'll be in trouble. I've never seen them play so sloppy as they did this weekend."

Weaver seemed to agree with Revering's assessment.

"We let them do their thing in this series," Weaver told the *Sun*. "I don't think we went after Henderson the right way. And we knew they were going to bunt on us, and they did."

Pitching coach Miller felt the O's offense let the club down.

"If you don't score, they play Billy Martin's game," Miller said. "It's a little bit embarrassing."

Baseball fans everywhere would wake up on Monday to find the Yankees lead had grown again. Rudy May was too much for his ex-employer, the Angels. He turned in seven scoreless frames for win No. 13. Gossage struck out Larry Harlow with a pair of runners on in the ninth for his 24th save. The Yanks' seventh win in a row went in the book as a 4-1 decision. May, who won a career high 18 games for the 1977 O's, knew not to forget about the slumping Orioles.

"It would be very, very depressing to me if I was over there," May told the *Times*. "But I know Earl Weaver and I know the guys. They're not going to give up. They know we are going to lose some games. That's why we have to keep playing hard. This thing ain't over yet."

Gossage echoed the same thoughts.

"I don't think any lead is a safe lead right now," Gossage said. "The Royals have a safe lead (18.5 games). But any lead we get is not safe unless we win every game and they lose every game. And that's not going to happen."

Stone's loss to Oakland put the Birds on shaky ground.

"I've got a feeling we're going to have a pretty good week now," Weaver said in the *Sun*. "Some fans are down, but they should take it easy, relax and wait until next Sunday. Let's see where we are when we come home again."

With 27 games to play, the Orioles still had plenty of time to make up some ground.

"I can't control the Yankees situation," Weaver continued. "I honestly felt they would lose more than they did during this stretch. But we've got no business losing three out of four, either. I would have been satisfied with seven of 11 here, but we didn't get it."

Crowley wasn't mailing in for his Yankees playoff tickets just yet.

"There is still plenty of time left," he said. "If we just play our game again, we'll be all right. We're struggling but if we go out and have a good road trip, we'll find ourselves right in the thick of things."

The second week of September would find the O's playing two games on Monday, the 8th. Dennis Martinez and Flanagan would get the nod for Baltimore. Detroit would opt for 13-game winner Milt Wilcox and 21-year-old Dan Petry. It was also a date for scoreboard watching. Gura would aim for win No. 19 in Calfornia. John would seek to become the third 20-game winner in the Majors, joining Stone (22) and the Phillies' Steve Carlton (21). John would face Dave Stieb in Toronto.

In game one, Seven O's doubles and three homers helped Martinez claim his fifth win of the year, 7-2. Both teams combined to strike out 20 times. In game two, Petry retired four Orioles batters in his brief outing. After two innings, Bumbry had two hit singles, scored two runs, and stole two bases. Flanagan had six early runs to work with. His 14th win and Stoddard's 20th save highlighted the doubleheader sweep. In the 8-6 win, 24 hitters struck out. Kiko Garcia took honors in this dubious category by fanning all four times.

Meanwhile in Canada, Bobby Murcer's 13th homer highlighted the Yankees first and gave John two quick runs to work with. And the left-hander retired the first nine Jays in order. However, the first four Toronto hitters reached base in the fourth, and Toronto scored three times. Stieb's lead was 4-3 heading to the visitor's last at-bats. That's when the Yanks first four hitters combined for a cycle. In order, it was a Murcer double, an Oscar Gamble triple, a Bob Watson single, and a Rick Cerone two-run homer. John jumped into the 20-

win circle for the third and final time of his 26-year run. Gossage struck out Lloyd Moseby and was rewarded with his 25th save.

In California, Disco Dan Ford's first at-bat against Gura resulted in his sixth homer of the season. Carney Lansford and Brian Downing also launched long balls versus the left-hander. Gura's 19th victory was not in the cards as he was charged with seven earned runs in less than five innings of work. His record dipped to 18-6 after the 7-4 defeat.

Stone's 22 victories was still tops in both leagues. Behind John's 20 victories stood three hurlers with 18 wins each. That group included Norris and Gura and a hard-throwing Indians right-hander named Len Barker. The 24-year-old was toiling in obscurity for the Indians, and on the 4th of July, his mark stood at 7-7. But as the Tribe embarked on a 14-day road trip, Barker's wins began to mount. A month later, he edged Norris and Oakland, 4-2 to move to 12-7. On Sept. 6, he beat Kansas City for the second time in three weeks to move to 18-8. Suddenly, the pitcher who would throw a perfect game against Toronto the following season was in the rear view mirror of the Cy Young race. Barker had also passed Norris to take the league lead in strikeouts with 159. Norris had also surrendered first place in the ERA race to New York's May.

Far from the maddening pennant chase on the East Coast, Norris would be opposed by steady left-hander Jon Matlack of Texas. Both pitchers gave their bullpens the night off. Norris was a little bit sharper and joined the 19-win club with a 3-1 decision.

Stone's 22 victories put him into some select company in Orioles history. It took nine seasons for Steve Barber to claim the first 20-win season in O's lore. The year was 1963. McNally was next in line (1968) and he set the club record at the time with a 22-10 mark. Two years later both McNally and fellow lefty Mike Cuellar moved that mark up to 24 victories. On Sept. 13, 1970, McNally registered win No. 23 in grand style, a 13-2 romp over the Red Sox. Two days later, Cuellar beat the Senators in Washington, 6-2. Both pitchers would lose decisions the next time out. Cuellar snared win No.24 on the 24th and set his sights on No. 25 on Sept. 29. He went eight strong innings and struck out 10. Senators' right-hander Joe Coleman was just as good. Mark Belanger's sacrifice fly won it in the 10th. Cuellar settled for a no decision. McNally beat the Senators on the next day for his 24th.

Both Orioles' Cy Young Award winners, Palmer (1975) and Flanagan (1979), fell one victory shy of the club record of 24 victories. Palmer won his 20th on the final game of August. Palmer out dueled New York's May for his 23rd win on Sept. 28.

Flanagan and the Indians' Dan Spillner would meet twice during the final week of the 1979season. Both pitchers would complete eight innings of work on Sept. 23. Flanagan allowed two hits. Spillner gave up 10 in the 3-1 O's win. The victory was the Orioles 100th of the season. In a bid for win No. 24, Flanagan struck out 11 Indians in Cleveland on the 29th. He took a 1-0 lead to the seventh. That's where he ran into pinch-hitter Cliff Johnson. The slugger's three-run homer was the biggest blow of the game and left Flanagan one win short of the club record for wins in a season.

Four-game series would kick off in Toronto and Boston beginning Thursday, Sept. 11. New York's Tiant would return to his home for eight years and battle Dick Drago at Fenway. Lefty Paul Mirabella would try to hold serve at Exhibition Stadium against the league's top winner, Stone. Of lesser importance to Orioles fans, Dennis Leonard would gun for win No. 18 in California.

Stone had not pitched against the Jays dating back to the last day of June. He notched win No. 11 that night, hurling seven scoreless innings. A subtle change in the Jays infield apparently paid dividends for the Birds. Speedy shortstop Alfredo Griffin nursed his bruised thigh and had his post filled by former O's farmhand Bob Bailor. Bailor's resume included just 13 at-bats in a Baltimore uniform before being drafted by the expansion Jays in 1977. The move north helped his career as he was the toughest player in the league to strike out in 1978. In the second inning, the man he couldn't beat out at shortstop, Belanger, spanked a ball toward him at short. Bailor gloved the ball but lost his footing and couldn't register the third out.

"If Bobby hadn't had his feet come out from under him, they would have been out of the inning" Stone told the *Toronto Star*.

With new life, Belanger broke for second on a steal attempt. DeCinces made a break for the plate. And pitcher Paul Mirabella froze on the mound. The Birds were on the board with the help of a rare double steal.

"Maybe he got rattled by the double steal," said Jays manager Bobby Mattick. "But a Big League ballplayer shouldn't be bothered by that sort of pressure."

Even against a southpaw, the O's ran at will against Mirabella and catcher Ernie Whitt. With three steals in the frame and some clutch hitting, the O's stormed to a 4-0 lead. In the home half, Stone issued a pair of two-out free passes. No hits went up on the home team board until the fourth. That's when Lloyd Moseby went the opposite way for a leadoff safety. Toronto put runners on first and second with no one out but Stone fanned Roy Howell for the second time in three innings.

The O's offense struck again in the sixth aided by two-baggers from Kelly and Dauer. Stone's working margin was now six runs. It was down to five after the sixth. Howell finally made contact and rapped a double of his own. With runners on the corners, Stone uncorked his fifth wild pitch of the campaign. This one was costly as Howell trotted home with his team's first run. Stone averted further trouble by fanning Willie Upshaw.

There was another Jays' uprising in the eighth. John Mayberry and Howell sprayed hits to the outfield and Upshaw drew Stone's fourth walk of the game. Garth Iorg started in left field for Toronto. After two fruitless at-bats vs. Stone, he gave away to left-handed swinging pinch-hitter Steve Braun. The former Twins regular bounced to Dauer in the seventh.

Joe Cannon opened up the eighth in left. But with a lifetime bat-ting average of .176, this dud of a cannon was not the player to stand in with the sacks loaded. In his place stepped in the left-handed Al Woods. In almost 2,000 at-bats, Woods powered 35 big league hom-ers. In 1980, he reached double figures in homers for the only time with 15. Stone fanned him leaving the bags loaded.

Stone would throw 142 pitches on this night. Those keeping track determined 82 were curveballs.

"He throws the curveball now when he gets behind on a hitter," Weaver said. "He's not using as many changeups as he used to. He'll rarely throw his forkball. He used to throw too many different kinds of pitches. Now, he'll throw as many as 70 curveballs a game."

The ninth inning was only notable as Bumbry laced his fourth single of the game. Damaso Garcia's two-out double, his 30th of the season, delayed the celebration only momentarily. Moseby popped one up and Belanger squeezed it for the final out. Stone earned his 23rd victory on foreign soil. In the route-going performance, Stone had walked four and struck out seven. Only Howell reached him for more than one hit, but Stone returned the favor by striking out the third baseman twice. The Majors' biggest winner was thinking about his team first on this night.

"This year as defending champions, I haven't noticed any tight-ness at all," Stone told the AP "This club has a lot of confidence and ability to keep in position to win ballgames. They're very assured of their own capabilities and we realize we are going to go out there and win as much as we possibly can. At this stage, that's quite often. There's really not much tension."

Speaking of tension, Stone told the press he was under very little strain on this night in Canada.

"When you are coming down to a pennant drive, there isn't any more pressure than there is during the rest of the season," Stone said. "I had a streak of 14 wins. I started the All-Star Game. And I pitched two games against the Yankees in a crucial eight-game series.

How can a game like this present any more pressure than the others?"

With the Stone win, the O's soared to 30 games over the .500 mark at 85-55.

"I'm with a team that enables me to win," Stone said. "If you come down to the seventh or eighth inning, they're not going to blow it. The truth is I go through extensive mental preparation before I pitch. I could always throw. The mental and the physical came together at the right time."

And when asked to explain what took him so long to figure things out, he was waiting with his answer in hand.

"Einstein didn't develop his theory of relativity overnight."

The O's would look to Boston for some help in slowing down the Yankees. The Sox were nearly a dozen games off the pace but that didn't stop nearly 33,000 from attending the latest edition of the the rivalry. They got their money's worth as nine pitchers and 10 innings later, the Yanks emerged with their 10th win in 11 games, 8-5. Bob Watson was the hero with a pair of homers, including a grand slam. Watson had given up a run with his glove early but certainly atoned for it with his bat.

"I caused a one-run deficit," Watson said. "And I just wanted to get one back. I knew when I hit it that it was going to at least hit the wall. I was halfway down the first base line when I knew it was going to be out."

Manager Howser felt he had the right guy at the plate.

"Watson played for the Red Sox last year and knows their pitchers better than anybody," Howser said. "He's our most consistent hitter even though he's been bothered by a broken finger on his left hand this season."

New York's lead in the East was three games.

"I pay no attention to it," Stone said told the *Toronto Star*. "I need all my attention to the team I'm pitching to. The thing is if we win, we can't lose any ground and if we lose there is nothing we can do that will affect the other game."

On Sunday the 14th, the O's offense consisted of just one player. Murray's 29th homer of the season tied the contest in the fourth inning in Toronto. His 30th homer forced another tie in the ninth inning. His 31st long ball opened the 11th inning and gave the O's a 3-2 lead.

That lead didn't last. Murray's three homers weren't enough in a 4-3 loss in 13 innings.

"I can't be happy about losing," Murray said. "Right now the Yankees have to lose for us to have a chance and they aren't losing. Getting into the World Series last year was my biggest thrill. It's going to be tough this time because we're not getting help from anyone."

Weaver tried to put a positive spin on the situation but he may have been reaching for the stars a little.

"When we left Baltimore, people said we were greedy to expect to win six of eight games," Weaver said. "As it turns out, it wasn't good enough to win six of eight. If New York wins 15 of 19 games, it doesn't matter what we do. Our job is to win the rest of our 19 games."

On Tuesday, Sept. 16, the 86-57 Birds would return to the states and head for Detroit. Stone would go for win No. 24 and the chance to tie both Mike Cuellar and Dave McNally for most wins in one season in club history. After a blistering 19-6 June, the fifth-place Tigers had played .500 ball the rest of the way and stood at a respectable 73-70. After Stone beat the team's ace, Morris on May 23, the Tigers right-hander won seven of his next eight decisions. But the streaky hurler was also riding a three-game losing streak into this game. Also on this night, the Yanks went home to battle the Blue Jays.

In Texas, Oakland's Norris would make an attempt at his first 20-win season. Like Stone, Norris had never come close to winning 20 games in the five prior campaigns. He would add just 23 more wins in his next 47 games. Following arm problems, he left the scene following the 1983 season at age 28.

Remarkably, he returned to the A's seven seasons later (1990) and appeared in 14 games. On April 17, 1990, Norris earned his first AL victory in seven seasons by hurling one inning of perfect relief. This A's club led by 27-game winner Bob Welch, won 103 games.

Alan Trammell laced a one-out double against Stone in the first. There were two runners aboard with just one out when Stone again received some help. First, he fanned Champ Summers. Trammell headed for third and unwisely tested the arm of Dempsey. The strike-him-out-throw-him-out twin killing snuffed out the visitor's rally just like that. In the second, Stone fanned both Lance Parrish and Al Cowens.

The O's offense zeroed in on Morris on the bottom half of the frame. Murray and Crowley played the doubles game and Birds went up a run. Dempsey aided his pitcher again in the third. Stone gave a free pass to leadoff hitter Rick Peters. The center fielder, who stole 13 of his career 20 bases in 1980, tried to move into scoring position before Dempsey made it 2-for-2 with another strike for the third out.

Bumbry led off inning three with a solo shot, his eighth homer of the campaign, and Stone had two runs to work with. Stone's sixth wild pitch of the season put a runner in scoring position in the fourth. He again escaped unharmed. By the sixth, he caught Trammell looking at strike three. Still, Peters stood on first base after a single.

Following the 1979 campaign, the Tigers knew they had something special going with former No. 1 draft pick Steve Kemp. In 1979, the 24-year-old slugger played in 134 games, scored 88 runs, hit three triples and stole five bases. He would finish the 1980 campaign after seeing action in 135 games, scoring exactly 88 runs, and again producing three triples and five stolen bases. In the two seasons combined, the southpaw slugger would hit 47 homers.

"Steve Kemp was a very good player," Stone told this writer.

His 19th roundtrip per of the season ended Stone's shutout bid and knotted the contest at 2-2.

Summers drew a free pass from Stone following the homer, and Stone was getting frustrated with the work behind the plate of umpire Russ Goetz.

"I had a wonderful curveball," Stone told the *Washington Post*. "But there was no strike zone for it. I told the umpire (Russ Goetz) there has to be a strike zone somewhere. High? Low? Just tell me where it is and I'll throw it there. He wouldn't call any curve a strike. When the plate is two inches by two inches for my best pitch then I might as well phone in the game."

Two O's reached base in the sixth but a double play grounder ended the threat. The top of the seventh proved to be Stone's undoing. Three consecutive hits and a bases loaded walk to Trammell put the Tigers ahead to stay. Tippy Martinez found similar trouble with Kemp and allowed a two-run single breaking the game wide open. The Tigers led 6-2. Detroit would win its 74th game of the season, 8-3.

Stone's sixth defeat of the season was his third in his last four outings at Memorial Stadium. That was in stark contrast to a streak of 21 wins in 23 decisions in Baltimore dating back to June of 1979.

Stone was clearly disappointed his best pitch didn't get any respect on this night.

"I thought I had as good control of the curve as I've had all year," Stone said in the *Baltimore Sun*. "And I walked five batters. I felt I should have shut them out. Goetz said they (curveballs) were too low, too high or too outside. It was a difference of opinion. I thought they were strikes. He thought they were balls. Unfortunately, he was the one calling them."

Weaver thought those curves danced over the plate as well.

"Steve had a good curve tonight," Weaver said. "But he (Goetz) was calling it a ball. And if you're not going to get it called a strike on the corners or down low, then you will have to come down the middle. Then, they were hitting it."

Was the pennant chase in the AL East over for this season? There were no white flags flying anywhere near this clubhouse.

"No, it's not over yet, gentlemen," Weaver told reporters. "We'll just have to put some wins together so they'll know we're here. The Yankees did what they had to do but we don't want to hand it to them. We'll have to put as many on the board as we can, so they'll hear some footsteps.

"It's the Yankees who are making things look so bad by playing so good. Any way you cut it, we've played well. They've just played better. Aw, the Yankees could mess it up. We might have a thrill yet. We've got to put some pressure on them and let them know we're still in it. Oops, I don't use the word pressure do I? We'll we've got to win some games in a row. It's going to be tough. The Yankees are going to have to have a funny streak. And they ain't been too funny lately."

Stone was not giggling at the prospect of a lost pennant either.

"Well," he said. "I think Ronald Reagan has a real good shot. Well, it appears the Yankees have a six-game lead. That about sums it up."

Stone reportedly threw 79 curves out of his 114 pitches.

The other Cy Young candidates were making strides while Stone slipped. In New York, the visiting Blue Jays chased starter Guidry in the seventh only to run headfirst into the flame-throwing Gossage. The Jays had the tying run on board when the Goose relieved and saved Guidry's slim lead. With nearly three innings of relief, his 28th save was in the books in the 5-4 win. The Yankees stood with baseball's best record at 92-52.

In Texas, Norris faced 45 Rangers. Amazingly, the second-leading strikeout pitcher in the league fanned only third baseman Dave Roberts during his 11-inning exercise. Pitcher Mike Norris retired pinch-hitter Jim Norris in the bottom of the 11th to register his 20th victory of the season.

After 145 games, Baltimore was six games back. The Yankees offense had tallied 42 more runs than the O's. In fact, Baltimore was fifth in runs scored (599). Playing exactly .600 baseball (87-58), the Orioles pitching staff had surrendered the fewest runs in the league (567).

With the pennant race all but over, John would go after personal glory on Thursday, Sept. 18. In New York, John was stingy. He went the distance. He didn't walk a soul. He allowed no earned runs. And he was deprived of his 22nd win. Winning pitcher Luis Leal walked five but allowed just two hits. Toronto, aided by errors by John and Randolph, prevailed 2-1. New York's lead had been sliced to a still-safe 5 games.

On Friday, the O's would look to Boston for some help again. The Red Sox (77-66) would spend the weekend in the Bronx while the O's would remain at home to play three games with the Blue Jays. In an attempt to tie the club record for victories, Stone would be opposed by Dave Stieb in the middle game of the series.

Saturday night's contest in Baltimore drew just 16,000 fans. At stake was a short chapter of Orioles' history. Stone would make a go at both McNally and Cuellar's record of 24 wins. Jays skipper Bobby Mattick presented a simple batting order. His infielders, (Alfredo Griffin, Garth Iorg, Roy Howell and John Mayberry) would bat first for Toronto. After designated hitter Steve Braun took his hacks, the three Jays outfielders (Lloyd Moseby, Bob Bailor and Paul Hodgson) would get their shot at Stone. Catcher Ernie Whitt would finish the attack.

Stone faced all four Toronto infielders in frame No.1. Mayberry fanned to close the inning. Iorg's single to right was wasted. Singleton batted with two on and none down and promptly produced two outs with a ground ball.

Murray's two out at-bat drove in Bumbry with the game's first run as the Birds struck first. The second inning found both pitchers finding their groove. After a free pass and a wild pitch, Stone fanned both Bailor and September call-up Hodgson. Stieb answered back with strikeouts of Graham and Crowley.

The action would pick up considerably in the fifth. The 62-85 Blue Jays would place two baserunners on with one down. Stone kept his slim margin when Iorg tested Singleton in right for the third out.

It was all but over following the O's fifth. Four singles, two walks and a Belanger double chased Stieb. Belanger and Singleton each earned two RBI in Stieb's unraveling. By the time southpaw Paul Mirabella was ready, five runs had already crossed. In the seventh, Stone surrendered one of Hodgson's nine career hits. However, the rookie Hodgson, a native of Montreal, was promptly erased from play when Dauer snared Whitt's line drive and earned two outs with the play.

Leading 6-0 entering the ninth, Stone prepared for some more personal history. He had never reached double figures in complete games and was just three outs short of his second consecutive nine-inning performance against the Jays. Mayberry was first up and he ended the shutout bid with his 27th homer of the season.

Braun had done nothing with Stone is three prior at-bats. But the former Twins regular drilled one to center for a clean hit. Still there was no danger of losing this lead. And then Weaver made his move. The left-hander (Martinez) was beckoned from the O's pen.

"I wasn't sorry to come out," Stone told the *Toronto Star*. "I was tired and it was very muggy for so late in the season. Besides, Toronto makes a habit of coming back lately. With Moseby coming up, a guy who can hit the ball out, the percentages were better with Tippy."

Toronto would get three of its seven safeties in the ninth. Stone had joined McNally and Cuellar in the O's record book with his 24th victory of the campaign. Plus, he had some extra incentive on this humid night. He spent part of his afternoon watching Gaylord Perry struggle in the Bronx. In front of more than 50,000 fans, Boston starter Dennis Eckersley went the distance and struck out eight Yanks. Boston kept the pennant chase in the East alive for at least a few more days, 4-1.

"We put pressure back on the Yankees," Stone told the *Star*. "I really feel good about the Orioles chances. I watched the final out at home. And I came to the park very confident. We have to take advantage of every Yankees loss."

Staring at a four-game Yankees lead, Stone answered questions regarding his personal and team goals.

"I think I have a shot to win the Cy Young Award," Stone said. "But every game I win is important — not only to me but to the team."

Now officially nine wins past his top win total in a single season, Stone could indeed ponder what it all meant.

"When you're a nine-year overnight success and you're having a season like I am, well it just doesn't get any better than this." Stone told *Newsweek*.

After 148 games of baseball, the Houston Astros and Los Angeles Dodgers stood exactly 84-64 and shared leadership honors of the NL West. The NL East race showed the Expos were 10 percentage points up on the second-place Phillies.

In the individual contests, Stone tied for top honors with teammate Flanagan and the Royals' Dennis Leonard in starts (34). Stone had slipped into a tie for fourth place in strikeouts (141) and was a distant second in free passes (96) to Toronto's Clancy. The workhorse Norris was tops in ERA (2.24) and second in strikeouts (159), complete games (21) and innings (257).

Norris would battle Leonard and the Western Division champion Royals on Sunday afternoon in Kansas City. And no matter that the pennant race had already been decided, more than 41,000 took this one in. Future O's third sacker Wayne Gross tagged Leonard for two homers and Norris had some rare run support to work with.

Naturally the right-hander went all nine innings to chalk up win No. 21. Leonard was tagged with seven earned runs in the same number of innings and fell short of his 20th win in the 9-3 lashing.

A Wednesday night crowd brought in more than 21,000 patrons to watch the host Orioles take on Boston. On line for Stone was a shot at his 25th victory. His control was not good on this Sept 24 night.

With Tony Perez's healthy track record against Stone, an intentional walk was ordered. Center fielder Garry Hancock was next. In his second season in Boston, Hancock was proving to be a batter who put the ball in play. In 115 trips to the plate, he walked just three times. That's one free pass for 39 times to the plate. During his six-year run in the majors, Hancock would walk once every 47 trips to the plate. Naturally, Stone walked him with the sacks full. Stone made a good pitch to Dwight Evans that induced a pop-out. But with two outs, he hit Boston rookie Chico Walker forcing in the third run.

Former Expos hurler Steve Renko was nursing a three-game losing streak entering this contest with the presumptive Cy Young Award winner. A Murray RBI single pulled the O's within two and Stone opened the second with two quick outs. And then Fisk bunted for a safety. And Rice singled bringing up Perez. Perez's 23rd homer of the year ended Stone's night with six earned runs in 1⅔ innings.

Even in the streak-ending loss in Texas, Stone had answered the bell for the third inning. Perez's blast had left the yard and Stone was finished for the night.

Trailing by five runs, the right-hander was in line for his eighth loss of the year. While Stone cooled off in the showers, his teammates heated up on the field. Both Bumbry and Dauer batted twice in the third inning. Crowley had the big blow of the frame, a three-run homer that chased Renko. Stone certainly must have known it was his year because before he grabbed a towel, he was off the hook. The O's had come all the way back to knot the game up at7-7. By the fourth, both Perez and Crowley had connected for their second long ball of the day. It stayed 9-9 until the seventh. This time, the three-run homer came off the bat of DeCinces. In a game of big blasts, relievers Martinez and Stoddard combined on 5⅔ innings of scoreless ball. Despite surrendering nine runs, the O's pitching staff remained the only club in the AL to have surrendered fewer than 600 runs.

Oakland's long-distance specialists were four runs behind in this listing but the A's offense had tallied more than 100 fewer runs therefore explaining the 15-game difference in the standings.

From the Bronx, there was a brief flicker of hope when visiting Cleveland struck first for a pair of runs in the second. Tiant settled in from there and the Yanks continued on their way with a 7-2 decision.

Norris was in the unaccustomed position of having plenty of runs to work with. The right-hander took a 7-2 lead to the fifth inning against the visiting Brewers on Friday night.

Even after allowing back to back homers off the bats of Yount and Cooper, he headed for another complete game. That final frame was enough to give anyone a headache. Norris surrendered seven Brewers hits including a solo homer from Gorman Thomas and an inside-the-park grand slam from Ben Ogilivie. Seven of the 17 Brewers safeties came in this five-run frame. Norris' preposterous line read: 9 IP, 17 H, 10 ER, 9 K and 4 homers allowed. In the 10-7 defeat, his ERA leaped from a league-leading 2.28 to second-place behind the Yankees Rudy May with a 2.52 mark.

Day games were popular on this Saturday. John looked for his 23rd win in Detroit against Jack Morris. Larry Gura was no doubt favored to claim win No. 19 in Minnesota. And Oakland's Rick Langford was in also in line for his 19th win against the Brewers.

Designated hitter Jim Lentine batted just over 200 times in his brief Major League stay. His career might have lasted a little longer if he had repeated his act on this day. Twice Lentine took John's pitches to the opposite field for safeties. John did not retire this California native once in Detroit's 5-1 win. It also helped the Tigers cause when catcher Lance Parrish tripled twice off the left-hander. John stayed two behind Stone in the win column, and the O's had staved off elimination for another day.

The Yanks' lead was 4.5 games with a week to play in the season. With an extra game to play, Baltimore would hope for a miracle while finishing with four in Fenway Park and three more at home against the Indians. The Yanks' six-pack would include two in Cleveland and the final four at home vs. Detroit.

Monday's twin bill in Boston would pit Dennis Martinez against Dick Drago in the first game. The second game would pit winless Keith MacWhorter against the league's top winner in Stone. Meanwhile, the Yanks would get the day off. Martinez went the distance for only second time this season in the 5-2 win. DeCinces and Dempsey hit back-to-back homers in the fourth.

Stone's second attempt at magical number 25 would again begin with fireworks before he took the mound in Boston. Five O's baserunners reached, and when Graham's opposite field sacrifice fly brought in Singleton, Stone was already up a pair of runs. Stone was clearly in uncharted territory coming in to this contest. His first pitch of the contest versus Rich Burleson would mark the start of his 243rd inning of 1980. This was 29 more frames than he had ever hurled in a single season (1975). Jim Rice's bat made note of that when the slugger singled in Dave Stapleton slicing the lead in half. Rice had been a major thorn in Stone's side since bringing his blistering lumber to the Big Leagues in 1974. Only in Rice's MVP season of 1978 did the slugger hit below .500 vs. Stone. His .568 career mark against Stone certainly stood out. His slugging percentage was off the charts at 1.162.

By the second, the Red Sox hitters were having flashbacks to five days earlier when they torched the Cy Young candidate. Chico Walker, who would later play parts of six seasons on the North Side of Chicago when Stone was working as the team's television analyst, opened the frame with a safety to center. Lefty catcher Rich Gedman pulled one to right and the corner bags were filled with no outs on the board.

It got worse in a hurry, shortstop Glen Hoffman put one in front of Bumbry in center and the game was tied at 2-2. The 23,000 at Fenway were preparing for another major uprising. DeCinces, at third, had other ideas. He scooped up a Dave Stapleton bouncer, touched third and fired to first for the final out. With new-found life, Stone even struck out his nemesis, Rice, in the third. In the fourth, Stone paid back both Walker and Gedman with third strikes. After a rocky start, both pitchers had settled down.

MacWorter had faced the minimum heading to the sixth. And he had a one-run cushion to work with. That's because both Rick Burleson and Stapleton had placed back-to-back doubles in the fifth giving the Sox a 3-2 lead. That advantage lasted two batters.

Singleton laced his third triple of the campaign into the right field corner. He trotted home when Murray went to the opposite field and over the Monster in left for this 30th homer.

Stone's last frame of his season came in the sixth and it was uneventful. Chico Walker coaxed the right-hander into a two-out walk. By the time he hung it up in 1993, Walker would take home 67 stolen bases. Not this time. Dempsey fired a strike to Garcia and Walker's stolen base attempt became the third out of the inning. Weaver would call for Sammy Stewart to finish the job.

Stone was certainly not brilliant in his 37th start of the season. But he was in a familiar place, leading 4-3 after six innings. He would be charged with three earned runs and seven Bosox safeties. Stewart was nearly flawless. In the eighth, Rice doubled and DH Dave Radar walked. Stewart simply struck out Dwight Evans to end the threat.

The bullpen stayed quiet in the ninth. Stewart also issued a free pass to the aforementioned Walker but he did not make second base, and the O's and Stone had a 4-3 win.

The only 25-game winner in Orioles history was born this Monday night in Boston. It was not Mike Cuellar, nor Dave McNally, nor Jim Palmer, nor Steve Barber, nor Mike Mussina, but rather Steve Stone.

"It's a good trivia question," Stone told this writer. "They never get to my name."

Twenty-five victories in one season has been rare the past 45 seasons. Beginning in the O's first World Championship year, 1966, Twins lefty Jim Kaat hit the 25-win mark during Minnesota's 89-win campaign. In 1968, of course, Detroit's Denny McLain won 31 games, the last time 30 was ever reached. The 1971 Tigers won 91 games and finished a good dozen games behind high-flying Baltimore. Mickey Lolich won 25 games that season. It seems almost impossible today but the workhorse Lolich started 45 games that season.

In 1974, the AL trotted out two 25-game winners in Oakland's Catfish Hunter and Texas' Ferguson Jenkins.

The Yankees' Ron Guidry won 25 of 28 decisions in 1978 and clearly was baseball's best pitcher that season. Magic No. 25 wasn't all that special in 1980. But that number has only been reached once in the 30 years since. Bob Welch reached the 25-win mark on Sept. 21, 1990. But he didn't stop there, beating both Kansas City and California to conclude a 27-win campaign.

The Senior Circuit has not had a 25-game winner since Steve Carlton won 27 games for the 59-win Philadelphia Phillies in 1972. Before that, Tom Seaver won 25 games for the Miracle Mets of 1969. Two years earlier, San Francisco's Juan Marichal won 26 games. And in 1966, the Dodgers' Sandy Koufax won 27 and the Marichal 25.

"Did I know what was coming?" Stone told this writer. "Lord knows, no. I really had a great 18 months. I went out 50 times and I lost only seven of them."

The O's had picked up a full game on the idle Yankees. Still, a 3.5 game deficit with 5 games to play didn't lend great optimism to O's fans.

"We're not out of it," Murray said. "We're not quitters."

"The lid remains ajar," Weaver said. "They can't close it tomorrow. People would forget the 1964 Phillies forever if we won it."

Ah, the 1964 Phillies. Sitting on top of the National League with a 6.5 game bulge on Sept. 20.

And then a 10-game losing streak. A sure pennant turned into a third-place finish.

"They've won more and lost fewer than us," Weaver continued. "Thinking about losing is not a good feeling. They're making us watch the scoreboard. But heck, watching the scoreboard, that's the fun of it. It's just that those guys for the last month have been losing up to the ninth inning and all the time winning."

That 3.5 game deficit was the exact margin the O's held over the Royals. With no wild card to bail them out, Baltimore players had to fill some satisfaction with having the Majors' second-best mark at 96 -61. On Tuesday, a Cy Young candidate was bombed and at the same time, maybe the Yankees did feel some pressure. The lead was down to 2.5 games at night's end. Indians catcher Ron Hassey had doubled and homered in the second inning alone. Cleveland put an eight-spot on the board. Of course, this seemingly safe lead didn't hold as the Yanks patiently took a 9-8 lead the eighth. And that lead was in safe hands as Gossage prepared his team for win No. 100.

It didn't happen.

Hassey had another run-scoring hit as Gossage blew a save and picked up his second loss in the 12-9 loss.

"We're still three up on them in the loss column," Dick Howser told the *Times*. "They have to come and get us. We can win tomorrow, or if we don't, we still have four at home."

In Boston, Singleton and Murray each had 3 hits in an 11-6 win. And Norris finally got some hitting support in Chicago. The right-hander moved to 22-9 on the campaign, despite three wild pitches bringing his season total to nine on the year. Oakland romped 11-3. Norris' seven strikeouts left him just one short of Len Barker, the league leader. His ERA rose just slightly to 2.53 as he settled permanently into second place behind Rudy May.

On Saturday afternoon, Detroit's Richie Hebner fanned on a blazer from Gossage. It marked the end of the pennant chase in the AL East.

"I had butterflies the whole game," the Goose admitted. "It's seldom that I get butterflies but in a game like this. You don't want to go into tomorrow. If we lost two today and Baltimore would sweep, we would find ourselves needing to win tomorrow. I just felt this was it, end it right now."

Flip forward 15 years. The Yankees would again head for postseason play. This time, however , it was via the inaugural wild card rule. With the second-best record in the Majors, the O's would have clinched a Wild Card back on Sept 17 and rested the regulars until they battled Kansas City. Instead, Baltimore could take some solace in winning 100 games.

Despite the Orioles not successfully defending their American League crown, their fans did have some reason to smile as the long winter season began to creep in.

First and foremost was the jerk of Gossage's head when George Brett turned around one of his speedballs.

Just short of 57,000 had sat through a 32-minute rain delay in Yankee Stadium. Lefty Tommy John nursed a 2-1 lead into the seventh inning of Game Three of the American League Championship Series with Kansas City.

Willie Wilson legged out a two-bagger and was the tying run when the Goose was called on to close out this rally. He didn't get U.L. Washington out, and more important, he didn't come close to stopping Brett. Yankees fans were stunned when Brett positively smoked a Gossage fastball.

"When Rich Gossage is pitching, you don't look for a change-up," Brett told the *Times*. "I'd been swinging bad. I thought I had been swinging bad all series. But I think I can hit speed as good as anybody."

The club the Orioles had chased for 162 games was knocked out in three straight games.

Gossage took the loss in the finale, a 4-2 decision.

"I feel I'm the best around and he's the best around," Gossage said. "He beat me that time. It just came at an awful time. It was the worst time."

In the National League, the Houston Astros were six outs short of claiming a National League flag in Game Four of the League Championship Series.

In the decisive Game Five, it again seemed over when Houston put a three-spot on the board in the seventh inning. But Nolan Ryan couldn't hold it in the eighth as Philadelphia tallied six, and the Phillies would head to their first World Series since the Whiz Kids of 1950. After four games, Willie Mays Aikens had four homers to his credit. Philly won the first two at home. Kansas City took the next two.

The Royals gave Quisenberry the ball to close out Game Five, but his blown save gave the Phillies a chance to clinch it at home behind 24-game winner Carlton. Pete Rose had three hits as the Phillies won 4-1 to win the World Series in six games.

On Nov. 4, Carlton completed his gorgeous campaign by securing his third Cy Young Award. Carlton notched 23 of 24 first-place votes and easily earned the award over runner-up Jerry Reuss of the Los Angeles Dodgers. Carlton would also finish sixth in the balloting for MVP, finishing behind teammate Mike Schmidt, who slugged 48 homers.

Despite his flirtation with the .400 mark, George Brett did not dominate the voting for AL MVP. Still, 17 first-place votes gave him a most comfortable win over Reggie Jackson (five). Gossage's 33 saves earned him four first-place votes and one tally went to Kansas City's Willie Wilson. Stone was a distant ninth.

Cleveland's Joe Charboneau and Los Angeles' Steve Howe took home the Rookie of the Year honors. Montreal's Bill Gullickson and Chicago's Britt Burns were named rookie pitchers of the year.

A week later, the writers' choice for the AL Cy Young winner would be announced. With his 22 wins and 24 complete games, Oakland's Norris felt he was a frontrunner in this close race.

He also knew his major competition would be the 25-game winner from Baltimore.

"Anybody who has won 22 games should have a good crack," Norris said. "But based on my stats, there's no doubt, I've done a better job than he has."

Stone could counter with a Major League-best 25 games won. Plus years later, Stone felt that since his games were pitched in the heart of a pennant chase, he was the most logical choice.

"We won 100 games and don't go to the playoffs," Stone told this writer. "There are only two teams in baseball history to do that. I was 14-1 against the AL East. Norris was 7-7. That's the toughest division in baseball. I won 14 in a row and 19 of 20. I won 25 games. I also beat the Yankees twice within a week."

Baseball writers studying simply statistics could naturally see Stone had three more victories and two fewer losses. Besides the Orioles, only the Yankees, Royals, Tigers, Red Sox, Brewers and A's posted winning marks in 1980. Against those clubs, Stone rang up a 12-3 mark. In personal matchups against division winners New York and Kansas City, Stone was a cool 5-1. On the other hand, Norris was a pedestrian 7-5 against those same clubs. He split four decisions against the Yanks and Royals. Neither pitcher had a losing record against any other team. Both pitchers liked to pick on the Blue Jays, collecting seven wins between them.

Gossage won 19 fewer games than Stone. But the fireballer saved a career-high 33 Yankees victories. Power pitching was his game. Remarkably, in 150 fewer innings than Stone, Gossage fanned just 46 fewer batters. Goose's ERA was also a full run better than the O's ace. MVP voters certainly understood the role of the closer as four writers made Gossage their top choice over George Brett.

Tommy John's 22-win season would certainly garner some attention in the Cy Young race along with Kansas City closer Dan Quisenberry's 33 saves as well as and Royals' starter Gura's 18 wins.

The voting was as close as expected. Both Stone and Norris each received 13 first-place votes. But in the overall voting, Stone scored 100 points to Norris' 91.

Stone was the second consecutive Orioles pitcher to earn the coveted Cy Young Award.

"You look at the names beside the Cy Young Award," he said. "My God, Jim Palmer, Tom Seaver, the superstars. Then, me, a .500 pitcher all my life. I thought maybe one day there would be a chance I'd get into a World Series and maybe into an All-Star Game. But the Cy Young Award? Never. That's what makes it so much sweeter. All the sweat. All the doubts. Tonight, we drink."

Stone could opt for an expensive martini on this night because Hank Peters owed him the cool $10,000 for copping the Cy Young Award.

Peters wasn't opposed to hand out this cash.

"The only comfort I have," Peters told the *New York Times,* "is the award can go to only one of them each year."

Stone tried to explain how his magical campaign came together. It was as if the stars all aligned all at once. But now that it was a reality, he wasn't backing down.

"All along, I thought I deserved it, and I'm sure Mike Norris thought he did. The decision in no way diminishes the type of season he had."

Years later, Stone is certain he was the deserving winner of the Cy Young Award.

"Three writers left Norris off their ballots," he said. "I guess he must have made someone mad. If I had had a vote, Norris would have been on it. It was a pretty close vote. But I would say the AL East was the toughest division in baseball. The Yankees had the best record in baseball. We won 100 games and finished second. Milwaukee had future Hall-of-Famers (Paul) Molitor, (Robin) Yount and also (Cecil) Cooper, (Ben) Ogilvie and (Gorman) Thomas, and they can't win. Boston had (Fred) Lynn, (Jim) Rice, (Carlton) Fisk and (Rick) Burleson. Their ninth hitter, Butch Hobson, hit 30 homers."

There was plenty of time for reflection when the announcement came out.

"There was no pressure during the 14-game winning streak because it kind of snuck up on me. I won a few and then had three no-decisions. Before I knew it, it was eight, nine and 10 in a row, and then came the All-Star break when I didn't think about the streak."

Gracious to the end, Stone knew he had plenty of folks to thank.

"Tim (Stoddard) and Tippy (Martinez) did an exceptional job. Without them, there's no way I would have won the award. When I get the trophy, I expect to see all three names engraved on it. I'm not the kind of guy who can go out and complete 25 games."

His press conference continued, perhaps setting the stage for a career behind a mic.

"Obviously this team can play," Stone said. "They have been great to me, great for me. Ray Miller, our pitching coach, is a great psychologist. Before, I would start a game and try to get all my pitches over in the first two innings. He told me that spoils your rhythm. Show them your curve early, maybe then the fastball later, then the slider later. Save something. Simple, but nobody ever told me that before. It's all confidence. I always thought I would win before coming to Baltimore, but I always had reservations. Now, I know I will win when I go out to the mound. I feel like I will win 30 next year. With this team behind me, how can you not?"

Stone's press conference continued with the right-hander recalling the toil and sweat from the past.

"A lot of people in Chicago said my career was over," he said. "One reporter wrote that I was finished and I told him if I made a successful comeback, I'd sauté the article. Every time I've had to progress to a higher league, they've said, 'Well,, he did it at this level, but he's not 6-foot-5, 200 pounds.'

"But I've learned that the ball still has to come in between the waist and the knees. "No matter where it starts from. I went out the last season and a half with a great amount of confidence. I truly believed I could win every time I went out to the mound."

As the calendar pushed towards December, Stone noted his bonus check hadn't been delivered as yet but he was not complaining.

"I didn't get the check yet," Stone said. "But that's not the most important part of the situation. I'm just pleased with the outcome. It's a great way to end the year. I'm relieved that it's finally out. I thought it was going to dragged out into next year. If you could write a script for a season, there's no way you could put more into it than I had this season. What's happened to me in Baltimore the last couple of years is fantastic.

"It can be an inspiration for a lot of guys who were in my position. But I decided a long time ago to get ready for reality after baseball. I realized way back that if it wasn't for my curveball, I might be serving filet instead of eating it.

"I have been taken from the ranks of journeyman and lifted to the pinnacle of my profession."

Stone won four more baseball games as member of the Orioles. He appeared in 15 more baseball games. His pitching elbow cried no more.

By 1982, he was out of baseball.

1980 Season

Final Standings

American League East	W	L	Pct.	GB
New York	103	59	.636	—
Baltimore	100	62	.617	3
Milwaukee	86	76	.531	17
Detroit	84	78	.519	19
Boston	83	77	.519	19
Cleveland	79	81	.494	23
Toronto	67	95	.414	36

Cy Young Award Voting

Name	Votes	1st Place Votes
Steve Stone	100	13
Mike Norris	91	13
Goose Gossage	37	2
Tommy John	14	0
Dan Quisenberry	7	0
Larry Gura	1	0
Scott McGregor	1	0

Cy Young Award Contenders

Player	W	L	S	ERA	G	IP	H	BB	SO
Steve Stone (Bal)	25	7	0	3.23	37	250⅔	224	101	149
Mike Norris (OAK)	22	9	0	2.53	33	284⅓	215	83	180
Goose Gossage (NY)	6	2	33	2.27	64	99	74	37	103
Tommy John (NY)	22	9	0	3.43	36	265⅓	270	56	78
Dan Quisenberry (KC)	12	7	33	3.09	75	128⅓	129	27	37
Larry Gura (KC)	18	10	0	2.95	36	283⅓	272	76	113
Scott McGregor (Bal)	20	8	0	3.32	36	252	254	58	119

Steve Stone Game By Game

Date	Opp	IP	H	R	ER	BB	SO	Decision	ERA
April 12	@CHI	5	7	3	3	1	1	L, 0-1	5.40
April 17	KC	7 ⅓	8	2	2	1	3	W, 1-1	3.65
April 25	@KC	1 ⅓	6	6	3	1	2	L, 1-2	5.27
April 30	NY	6 ⅓	5	3	2	5	0	W, 2-2	4.50
May 5	MIN	4 ⅔	5	4	3	4	2	L, 2-3	4.74
May 9	@MIL	6 ⅔	7	2	2	3	2	W, 3-3	4.31
May 13	TEX	8 ⅓	7	2	2	1	3	W, 4-3	3.86
May 19	@CLE	8 ⅔	6	1	1	1	6	W, 5-3	3.35
May 23	DET	8	3	3	2	3	6	W, 6-3	3.20
May 27	CLE	5	5	5	4	2	3	ND	3.52
June 2	MIL	5	9	5	5	2	2	ND	3.93
June 8	@CAL	3	6	5	5	2	2	ND	4.41
June 12	@SEA	9	6	1	1	5	6	W, 7-3	4.02
June 17	CAL	9	5	3	2	4	11	W, 8-3	3.81
June 21	SEA	9	5	0	0	2	7	W, 9-3	3.46
June 26	TOR	9	6	1	1	2	9	W, 10-3	3.25
June 30	@TOR	7	5	0	0	4	2	W, 11-3	3.04
July 4	BOS	6 ⅔	8	3	3	2	3	W, 12-3	3.10
July 12	KC	7	3	1	1	6	6	W, 13-3	3.00
July 16	@MIL	7 ⅓	9	4	4	1	5	W, 14-3	3.11
July 21	@MIN	7 ⅔	7	4	4	6	7	W, 15-3	3.19
July 26	MIL	7 ⅓	8	1	1	1	1	W, 16-3	3.09
July 31	@TEX	3	8	6	3	1	3	L, 16-4	3.21
Aug. 5	CHI	7	6	2	2	1	1	W, 17-4	3.18
Aug. 9	@NY	9	7	2	2	4	5	W, 18-4	3.12
Aug. 14	NY	9	2	1	1	5	3	W, 19-4	3.01
Aug. 19	@CAL	7 ⅓	2	2	1	4	6	W, 20-4	2.94
Aug. 23	@OAK	6 ⅓	3	2	2	2	6	W, 21-4	2.94
Aug. 29	CAL	4 ⅔	7	5	4	4	3	L, 21-5	3.05
Sept. 3	SEA	9	4	1	1	2	3	W, 22-5	2.96
Sept. 7	OAK	9	8	5	5	2	5	L, 22-6	3.05
Sept. 11	@TOR	9	8	1	1	4	7	W, 23-6	2.96
Sept. 16	DET	6 ⅓	7	6	6	5	5	L, 23-7	3.12
Sept. 20	TOR	8	6	1	1	3	5	W, 24-7	3.05
Sept. 24	BOS	1 ⅔	6	6	6	2	0	ND	3.26
Sept. 29	@BOS	6	7	3	3	2	4	W, 25-7	3.29
Oct. 4	CLE	7	7	1	1	1	4	ND	3.23

About Bill Pemstein

Growing up in the Washington, D.C., suburbs, Bill Pemstein naturally was attracted to the Washington Senators. However, the Senators decided to trade away his favorite player, Bob Johnson, up the road to Baltimore. That's when Pemstein's older brother used the opportunity to change his brother's allegiance to the Orioles. By the time Frank and Brooks Robinson hit back-to-back home runs off of Don Drysdale in Game One of the 1966 World Series, Pemstein was an Orioles fan forever.

After a five-year stint selling group and season tickets to Orioles fans in the Washington area, Pemstein moved to the Chicago area and became a sportswriter for Pioneer Press newspapers in north suburban Chicago. He currently is a freelance writer for the Arlington Heights (Ill.) *Daily Herald* and Patch.com. He has also served as a sports information director at Harper College.

Pemstein lives in Lake Zurich, Ill., with his former softball star wife and three sons, naturally named after former Orioles players.

He also is author of the blog *Let's Find H-Man a Wife* (http://hmanwifesearch.blogspot.com).

www.ingramcontent.com/pod-product-compliance
Lightning Source LLC
Chambersburg PA
CBHW021224090426
42740CB00006B/376